T0358193

# Cambridge Elements ≡

Elements in Ancient Egypt in Context
edited by
Gianluca Miniaci
*University of Pisa*
Juan Carlos Moreno García
*CNRS, Paris*
Anna Stevens
*University of Cambridge and Monash University*

# HIEROGLYPHS, PSEUDO-SCRIPTS AND ALPHABETS

## *Their Use and Reception in Ancient Egypt and Neighbouring Regions*

Ben Haring
*Leiden University*

CAMBRIDGE
UNIVERSITY PRESS

Shaftesbury Road, Cambridge CB2 8EA, United Kingdom

One Liberty Plaza, 20th Floor, New York, NY 10006, USA

477 Williamstown Road, Port Melbourne, VIC 3207, Australia

314–321, 3rd Floor, Plot 3, Splendor Forum, Jasola District Centre,
New Delhi – 110025, India

103 Penang Road, #05–06/07, Visioncrest Commercial, Singapore 238467

Cambridge University Press is part of Cambridge University Press & Assessment,
a department of the University of Cambridge.

We share the University's mission to contribute to society through the pursuit of
education, learning and research at the highest international levels of excellence.

www.cambridge.org
Information on this title: www.cambridge.org/9781009400794

DOI: 10.1017/9781009400800

First published 2023

*A catalogue record for this publication is available from the British Library*

ISBN 978-1-009-40079-4 Paperback
ISSN 2516-4813 (online)
ISSN 2516-4805 (print)

# Hieroglyphs, Pseudo-Scripts and Alphabets

## Their Use and Reception in Ancient Egypt and Neighbouring Regions

Elements in Ancient Egypt in Context

DOI: 10.1017/9781009400800
First published online: November 2023

Ben Haring
*Leiden University*
Author for correspondence: Ben Haring, b.j.j.haring@hum.leidenuniv.nl

**Abstract:** The Egyptian hieroglyphic script was exceptionally versatile, as becomes clear when studying its multiple uses both within Ancient Egypt and beyond its borders. Even the few cases discussed in this Element demonstrate that in the ancient world, hieroglyphs appealed to a wide readership, which ranged from highly accomplished scribes, artists and priests, to semi-literate workmen, as well as to speakers of non-Egyptian languages. Creative processes within these different groups resulted in very different adaptations of regular hieroglyphic writing: highly specialized enigmatic compositions, less-informed ad hoc orthographies, isolated uses of hieroglyphs as marks and emblems and the development of new writing systems. Important reasons for the wide appeal and deep impact of hieroglyphic writing are the iconicity and cultural messages of its individual signs on the one hand, and its remarkable semiotic strategies in rendering human language on the other.

**Keywords:** alphabets, Egyptian hieroglyphs, literacy, marking systems, pseudo-script

ISBNs: 9781009400794 (PB), 9781009400800 (OC)
ISSNs: 2516-4813 (online), 2516-4805 (print)

# Contents

# 1 Introduction

In the late fourth century AD, the last hieroglyphic inscriptions were carved on the walls of the Egyptian temple of Philae, in the deep south of Egypt. The latest hieroglyphs that can be dated precisely are from AD 394 (Devauchelle 1994; see Figure 1). They followed the rules of an especially intricate variant of the hieroglyphic script that had been current among Egyptian priests under Ptolemaic and Roman rule, a code used to record and transmit expert knowledge regarding Egyptian temple religion which had been accumulated over thousands of years within a narrow priestly circle.[1] Indeed, by AD 394, its readership had become so narrow that an explanatory note in a more widely known Egyptian script, Demotic, was added on the same wall, beneath the columns of hieroglyphs.[2] Demotic, a cursive script distantly related to hieroglyphs, would come to an end not much later, in the mid-fifth century AD, in the same Philae temple. At that point, the traditional pharaonic scripts gave way to alphabetic Greek, which had been used increasingly in Egypt since the early third century BC and which inspired the creation of the Coptic alphabet that would henceforth be used for writing the native Egyptian language, itself also heavily influenced by Greek (Quack 2017).

The traditional scripts that had been used in Egypt for thousands of years fell into oblivion. The principles of hieroglyphic writing and its cursive variants, hieratic and Demotic, would not be rediscovered until the early nineteenth century AD, when scholars such as Antoine Silvestre de Sacy, Johan Åkerblad, Thomas Young and especially Jean-François Champollion made the first significant steps towards the decipherment of the Ancient Egyptian scripts and an understanding of their language (Parkinson 1999: 12–45). Egyptologists regard the work of Champollion in particular as the birth of their specialism as a scholarly field in its own right. From that point onward, it would take many more years of research to elucidate the intricate workings of the hieroglyphic script. Today, that script and its various uses are largely understood by Egyptologists, although the grammatical principles of the older stages of the Egyptian language, Old and Middle Egyptian, remain hypothetical to a considerable degree (see e.g. Loprieno 1995: 8–10; Allen 2014: 455–62).

For the purpose of this Element, it is significant that, during the almost 1,500 years between their last use as an active writing system and their modern-day decipherment, hieroglyphs retained considerable graphic and symbolic appeal

---

[1] See Section 3.2 for this particular variant of the hieroglyphic script, called 'Ptolemaic'.

[2] It is, in fact, the Demotic text that supplies the date, a 'year 110', referring to an era counting from the accession of Emperor Diocletian in 284. Initially an era introduced by the Egyptian priesthood, it became the 'Era of the Martyrs' in Coptic Christianity and is still used as such today (Cannuyer 2018).

**Figure 1** The last dated hieroglyphic inscription, with Demotic text underneath.
After Griffith (1935–7: pl. LXIX)

to audiences from different cultures and periods. Middle Eastern and European intellectuals and artists, in particular, felt attracted to Egyptian hieroglyphs and their mysteries (Iversen 1993; El-Daly 2005: 57–73). Symbolic explanations of hieroglyphs have been proposed since late antiquity, the most widely known compilation being *The Hieroglyphics of Horapollo*. This Greek text was purportedly translated from an Egyptian original, and in Latin translation it enjoyed great popularity in the learned circles of Renaissance Europe with their thirst for allegory and emblematic images (see Boas 1993 for an English translation with illustrations).[3] Although many of the explanations given, indeed several of the 'hieroglyphs' themselves, seem to have non-Egyptian origins, the work is currently thought to include much authentic priestly knowledge of the last centuries of pharaonic religion (Iversen 1993: 48; Leal 2014). *Hieroglyphics* is certainly among the most direct sources for premodern scholarship on Ancient Egypt and its writings, whose tradition was otherwise dominated by

---

[3] The original date and authorship of the text (divided into two books) are uncertain. Its attribution to a grammarian or a philosopher named Horapollo of the fourth or fifth century AD may be pseudepigraphic; Fournet (2021) argues that *Hieroglyphics* as we know it was composed much later, while being based on ancient sources, mainly the first-century AD *Hieroglyphics* of Chaeremon of Alexandria.

classical Greek and Roman texts. The words referring to the different pharaonic monumental and cursive scripts – 'hieroglyphic', 'hieratic' and 'Demotic' – are illustrative of that tradition.[4]

Today, Egyptian hieroglyphs survive as symbols in artistic and popular imagination, even as emoji in digital communication. A splendid example is ☥, which retains much of its Ancient Egyptian meaning (*ankh* 'to live' and related words) in its modern uses. The purpose of the present Element is not to discuss the use of hieroglyphs in post-pharaonic scholarly and popular traditions, however interesting in themselves they may be. The principal aim is to show how and why hieroglyphs (and to a lesser extent, hieratic and Demotic) also enjoyed popularity outside a narrow circle of professional scribes and priests *during pharaonic history*. After discussing the ways in which hieroglyphs were used by Egyptian scribal and priestly specialists, the focus will be on uses of hieroglyphs by non-specialists, from apprentice or amateur scribes and draughtsmen, and semi-literate workmen, to the inventors of non-pharaonic codes and scripts partly inspired by Egyptian hieroglyphs. By examining a number of relevant examples, one can deduce what made hieroglyphs attractive to non-specialists and how they were used to develop different types of graphic communication, some of which may be called writing, while others were limited to using individual signs in isolation or to accumulations of signs that may appropriately be called 'pseudo-script'. Together, these widely different case studies will reveal aspects of the impact the hieroglyphic script had on individuals and societies in Ancient Egypt and its surroundings.

## 2 Hieroglyphs, Hieratic and Demotic: The Work of Specialists

Egyptian hieroglyphic writing was developed in the last centuries of the fourth millennium BC and the first centuries of the third. Isolated signs or small groups of them, appearing on tags of bone, ivory and wood from the thirty-third century BC, are regarded by some Egyptologists as (proto-)hieroglyphs. But their supposed phonetic reference is the subject of debate, and the use of hieroglyphs to record entire sentences in Egyptian only emerged slowly during the course of the Early Dynastic Period, circa 2900–2600 BC (Vernus 2016: 109; Stauder 2022: 251).[5] To be clear about what is meant by 'writing', the latter notion is

---

[4] From the Greek *grammata hieroglyphika* 'sacred carved letters', *hieratikos* 'priestly' and *grammata demotika* 'popular letters', respectively.

[5] The tags are those from tomb U-j in the cemetery of Umm el-Qaab; basic edition in Dreyer 1998. The signs on them are also known from rock inscriptions (e.g. Darnell 2017), sculpture and prestige objects found elsewhere in Egypt. For a critical appraisal, see Baines 2004 and Vernus 2016: 117–24. According to Stauder (2022: 227–31), the signs do not belong to a writing system but to a formal visual code that would start including phonetic notation in the decades after the U-j deposits. For the palaeographic development of the earliest hieroglyphs, see Regulski 2010.

understood here as the graphic or material encoding of utterances in a specific human language, including the indication of sounds of that language.[6] It is interesting to see that signs resembling the characters of what would become hieroglyphic writing made their first appearance in isolation as a means of expressing notions such as kingship, deities and perhaps the names of individuals, institutions or places. Such emblematic uses would remain an important characteristic of hieroglyphs throughout their history, in addition to their role as characters in written texts (see Section 3.1).[7]

Throughout the Pharaonic and Greco-Roman Periods of Egyptian history, hieroglyphs would be the script for monumental texts, occurring chiefly on stone surfaces, but also on objects of metal and wood, as well as on papyri. For the last, however, more cursive scripts would be developed that allowed the writing of administrative, religious and literary texts to be quicker. In the early third millennium BC, painted cursive hieroglyphs would develop into hieratic, a script with distinctive characteristics that set it apart from hieroglyphs, the most obvious being ligatures, the graphic joining of characters that is found in so many handwriting systems worldwide. Another feature is the orientation of hieratic characters, which invariably face right, with the consequence that hieratic texts are always read from right to left. The same orientation and reading direction were the usual ones in hieroglyphic writing, but since this script was mainly used to inscribe monuments, there was potential for hieroglyphic signs to be mirrored, as a means of adapting the texts and their reading order to the architectural or iconographic context. (This, for instance, could occur in units of text placed symmetrically on either side of a doorway, or in captions which adhere to the orientation of pictures they refer to.) A third important characteristic of hieratic is, obviously, the development of its own graphic shapes of signs, which in time became ever more simplified with respect to their corresponding hieroglyphs and, as opposed to the latter, lost much of their iconicity. Between monumental hieroglyphs and hieratic is another type of writing, called cursive or semi-cursive hieroglyphic. The characters of this script, which was mainly used for funerary texts on papyri and wooden coffins, are somewhat simplified when compared with their monumental equivalents. A feature they share with hieratic is that the signs are not reversed, but consistently face right, and so are to be read from right to

---

[6] Definitions in this sense are often given in grammatological literature – for example, Daniels 2018: 126. Sound, however, is not necessarily the single aspect of language that is referred to by writing. Logograms refer to words of a language, with or without additional phonetic specification (see Section 2.1 and Robertson 2004: 20–1).

[7] For the different semiotic modes among which writing emerged, see Morenz 2004, Vernus 2016 and Stauder 2022.

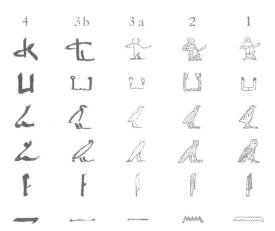

**Figure 2** Monumental hieroglyphs (nos 1–2), cursive hieroglyphs (3a–b) and hieratic (4). From Fischer 1979: 41. Copyright © 1979 The Metropolitan Museum of Art, New York. Reprinted by permission.

left.[8] See Figure 2 and Fischer (1979: 39–44) for the scripts mentioned in this paragraph.

By the seventh century BC, another cursive script had developed, which may have originated from a particular form of hieratic current in northern Egypt. That later script is called Demotic, and as we have seen in the Introduction, it was in use until the mid-fifth century AD, outlasting hieroglyphs by only half a century. The hieratic script, which remained in use together with Demotic, is attested until the third century AD (Wente 2001: 210; Grandet 2022: 69).[9] In the last millennium of its existence, it came to be reserved for religious texts – hence its Greek designation *hieratikos*, distinguishing it from the 'popular' Demotic script. However, the latter's use, which was initially administrative, could also be extended to religious and literary domains.

Writing any of these scripts was the specialization and prerogative of a tiny elite minority of Ancient Egyptian society: administrators, priests and artists. It is assumed that 1 or 2 per cent of the population at most attained full literacy in pre-Hellenistic Egypt, and this was mainly in a cursive script (hieratic or Demotic), for use in administrative duties (Ray 1994: 64–5; Baines & Eyre 2007: 64–7). The hieroglyphic script, by virtue of its monumental and decorative uses, was the specialization of an even smaller group, that of draughtsmen

---

[8] Funerary texts frequently reverse the order of vertical columns in which cursive hieroglyphs are written, but *within* the columns, the normal writing and reading direction is observed.

[9] A variant of hieratic called 'abnormal hieratic' was in use for administration and literature in southern Egypt together with Demotic until the late sixth century BC (Donker van Heel 2022: 70–1).

and sculptors. These specialists also mastered the cursive writing used by a wider circle of literati, but the reverse was not true: most of the people who read and wrote hieratic or Demotic would not have been capable of composing an error-free hieroglyphic text. The fact that knowledge of the cursive scripts was more widely spread than hieroglyphic expertise becomes clear in hieroglyphic inscriptions produced by less-accomplished artists, where cursive, semi-cursive or pseudo-hieroglyphic forms and groupings of signs appeared when the correct hieroglyphic versions did not come to the writer's mind. This would not normally happen in workshops of the royal residence, but it could and did occur in regional and local workshops producing private monuments (e.g. Haring 2010: 33–4). This was especially the case in periods without centralized kingship, and it had the potential to lead to orthographic innovations (see e.g. Vernus 1991). Drafts in hieratic and cursive hieroglyphic may have been important in the preliminary stages of the composition of hieroglyphic texts, but examples in monumental hieroglyphs were also available on papyri and ostraca (Haring 2015a; Laboury 2022b: 43–6). It remains unclear, however, how exactly draughtsmen went about composing fresh hieroglyphic texts.

## 2.1 Hieroglyphs As Characters of Writing: Sound and Meaning

The Egyptian hieroglyphic script is a complex mixture of phonetic and ideo-graphic writing, and the same is true for hieratic and Demotic, which follow the same basic principles.[10] A hieroglyphic sign can be used to express only sound (e.g. the owl 𓄿 for *m*, not for 'owl'), it can transmit meaning without sound (e.g. the sealed papyrus scroll 𓏞 can denote various scribal and mental activities and their products, and abstract notions), or it can express both sound and meaning at the same time (e.g. a cow's ear 𓄔 for *sḏm* 'to hear'). Hieroglyphic orthographies for words of some length (mostly nouns and verbs) often include signs of all three categories – for example, 𓄔 *sḏm* 'to hear/listen'.[11] This spelling includes, from right to left, a logogram (the ear, sound and meaning of the verb 'to hear'), a phonogram[12] (the owl, sound *m* only) and a determinative (papyrus scroll, category of meaning: mental activity). It is, in fact, the most common way to write this verb in hieroglyphic as well as in cursive texts. But its orthography can vary, especially in hieroglyphic, so that the same verb may also

---

[10] This section mainly serves to explain the principles of hieroglyphic writing to a non-Egyptological audience.

[11] The characters of Egyptological transliterations like *sḏm* are approximations (at best) of the sounds of spoken Egyptian. Ancient Egyptian scripts basically express consonants only; see Section 2.1.2.

[12] Also called 'phonetic complement' or 'phonemographic interpretant' (the latter term was introduced by Frank Kammerzell; Polis & Rosmorduc 2015: 167–8), since it is used to support the interpretation of an adjoining sign, in this case, the preceding logogram.

be written 𓀁𓃭𓅱, with the determinative 𓀁, a sitting man with a hand raised to his mouth to indicate oral or mental activity, instead of ⸺. Since the signs used in a full orthography overlap in meaning (logogram and determinative) and in sound (logogram *sḏm* and phonogram *m*), the verb can also be abbreviated to just one sign: the logogram 𓄔. Such variability is highly convenient when arranging hieroglyphs within the spatial confines of lines or columns on a wall or a statue; it is less urgent in texts written in *scriptio continua* on papyrus. The latter offer more space for full writings. What is more, because the cursive scripts have simplified forms that make the identification of individual signs difficult, they favour full, standardized orthographies which help the writer and reader to recognize words.

This would appear to be Ancient Egyptian orthography in a nutshell, but the accurate taxonomy of hieroglyphs and the principles of their use are more complicated than the examples given here might suggest (for an overview and discussion, see Polis & Rosmorduc 2015). To begin with, the terminology used here (phonogram, logogram, determinative) includes only three words of a more extensive vocabulary used by Egyptologists when discussing hieroglyphic writing. The category of signs called 'logogram' in the preceding paragraph, for instance, is otherwise called 'ideogram' or 'radicogram'. The former word is also applied to determinatives and indicates the capacity of both logograms and determinatives to express meaning directly through their pictorial quality, without phonetics in between (as opposed to the fully phonetic English orthography used to write this Element). For the same reason, they may also be called 'semograms'. The word 'determinative' will be discussed later in this section.

The word 'radicogram' (introduced by the Egyptologist Wolfgang Schenkel) would seem to be a more appropriate term than 'logogram', since it most often applies to the stem or 'root' (*radix*) of a word, rather than to one word specifically.[13] This becomes apparent from the previously mentioned example of 𓄔 in *sḏm* 'to hear', since the different possible inflections of this root, resulting in different words (e.g. 𓏏𓃭𓄔 *sḏm.n* 'we hear', 𓇋𓂝𓏤𓃭𓄔 *sḏmw.s* 'she is heard'), all use the same sign. Thus, the 'logogram' or 'word-sign' does not necessarily express a word, although it may do that when used autonomously – that is, for the writing of one specific word, when it includes no additional signs (Polis & Rosmorduc 2015: 166). Such autonomous use may be made explicit by one particular sign: the so-called stroke determinative, a

---

[13] In Egyptology as in Semitic studies, word bases are called 'roots' (referring to a string of consonants) rather than 'stems' (including consonants and vowels, as in European languages), since in Egyptian and Semitic languages, vowels *within* a root/stem follow the inflected form. Compare the root *qtl* in the classical Hebrew *qaṭōl* 'to kill' (infinitive), *qaṭal* 'he killed' (perfect), *qaṭūl* 'killed' (passive participle), *qoṭēl* 'who kills' (active participle).

simple vertical stroke ı which is also used to denote the number '1'. Thus, the human face combined with this stroke ı♀ means *ḥr* (/ḥ/ followed by /r/) 'face'. Without it, it can be used (and is very often used) phonetically for *ḥr* in words which incorporate these two consonants, whether or not these have anything to do with the human face. To complicate things further, the same group ı♀ is used for the preposition *ḥr* 'on'. It is quite possible that this preposition is related to the word *ḥr* 'face', but it functions as a different word, and so even the 'autonomous' sign is capable of being semantically ambiguous, a 'radicogram' rather than a 'logogram'. To be more precise, the radicogram is not autonomous at all: it represents a sequence of consonants, not necessarily a lexical unit (lexeme). Polis and Rosmorduc (2015: 157, 166–7) therefore propose to distinguish between non-autonomous radicograms and autonomous logograms, the latter referring to lexemes as well as to clusters of consonants.

It should have become clear by now that the taxonomic terms refer to functions of signs in context, not to the signs themselves as graphically defined (graphemes). The same grapheme may be phono-, logo- or radicogram, or determinative, depending on its position in a string of signs and on its intended meaning there. The 'autonomy' mentioned in the previous paragraph is relative. A sign's meaning depends on its position in the string – that is, on its syntagmatic relations with the surrounding signs. Only in combination do hieroglyphs represent human language, according to the principle of double articulation that characterizes writing systems in general: signs that are 'meaningless' in themselves, such as alphabetic characters, acquire linguistic meaning only when combined with other signs. Sign systems other than writing include systems of single articulation in which individual signs convey meaning directly by themselves as, for instance, marks and emblems.[14] 'Meaningless' is not to be taken in an absolute sense. Characters of writing can be used in isolation and still have meaning. This is even true for the abstract alphabetic characters used to type this text although, when used individually, they still refer to linguistic sounds, often as abbreviations of words (e.g. P for 'parking'), or with reference to the characters' positions in alphabetic sequence (e.g. for the purposes of numbering or grading). Pictorial signs like hieroglyphs present many more possibilities for autonomous use. We will see some important examples of this in later sections of this Element (especially Sections 4.2 and 5.1).

In addition to being part of systems of double articulation, characters of writing tend to be relatively closed sets of signs – that is, there is a more or less fixed repertoire of signs in a writing system. In alphabetic writing systems,

---

[14]  For single and double articulation, see, for example, Nöth 1990: 237, Depauw 2009b: 207–8 and Haring 2018: 91–2.

this principle seems fairly rigid: the English alphabet has twenty-six characters and users are not at liberty, in principle, to add more.[15] Pictorial writing systems like Egyptian hieroglyphs appear to be more flexible. Although a certain set of current signs existed and had to be mastered by users of the script, new signs could marginally make their appearance for ad hoc use, and could even become 'canonized' and kept in the repertoire for centuries.[16]

Determinatives especially represent a category open to the invention of new graphs. Determinatives are often generic, so as to be applicable to broad semantic categories of words. The papyrus scroll ▱, used for categories which one might label as 'abstract', 'mental' and 'written', is a fitting example. On the assumption that their function is the same as or similar to that of classifiers in spoken languages (even though Egyptian itself was not a classifier language), some Egyptologists prefer to use the latter term instead of 'determinatives' (e.g. Goldwasser 2002; Lincke & Kammerzell 2012; Polis & Rosmorduc 2015: 157–8, 165–6). The notion has been taken even further by Orly Goldwasser, who argued that classifiers reflect categorization ('knowledge organisation') in the minds of Ancient Egyptian speakers and scribes. The theory is attractive and has been admirably presented, with much supporting evidence (Goldwasser 2002), but it has also met with reservations. Eliese-Sophia Lincke and Frank Kammerzell, although in favour of the analogy of linguistic and written classifiers, do not see the latter as a 'reflection of mind', but as a 'result of sign usage' (Lincke & Kammerzell 2012: 80). There is perhaps no better illustration of this than the differences between the uses of determinatives/classifiers in the highly pictorial hieroglyphic script on the one hand, and in its cursive pendants, hieratic and Demotic, on the other.[17] Overall, the way these scripts select and deploy determinatives appears to be very similar, but in monumental hieroglyphs, often very specific determinatives are

---

[15] There are exceptions, of course, such as words borrowed from other languages featuring characters typical for non-English alphabets (e.g. ç in façade), or the use of additional signs, including pictograms, in (electronic) informal writing (e.g. emoji).

[16] It is difficult to say what exactly that set would have been for users of the hieroglyphic script at any point in Egyptian history. The repertoire of hieroglyphic font types established by Alan Gardiner (1957: 438–548) represents the current set accepted by Egyptologists, although its 769 graphs include rare signs and different graphic variants of the same signs, often from different periods. It concentrates on Middle and early New Kingdom repertoires (appr. 2000–1300 BC); its graphic forms are mainly inspired by monumental hieroglyphs of the Eighteenth Dynasty (1539–1292 BC). More extensive lists include the increased hieroglyphic repertoires of the Late and Greco-Roman Periods – for example, Daumas 1988–95; Grimal, Hallof & Van der Plas 2000; see Section 3.2. Collombert (2007), justly critical about quantitative inferences made from modern sign lists, arrives at a total of circa 1,500–2,000 signs for the Old Kingdom, but estimates a more restricted set of truly current signs at circa 600.

[17] This is in addition to the graphic differences between the hieroglyphic signs and their supposed cursive counterparts, not only in the degree of cursiveness or simplification, but also in what they actually represent; see Meeks (2015: 41–2).

employed (including signs which visually represent the signifieds of the preceding words, so-called repeaters),[18] whereas cursive scripts more often favour
generic signs.[19] One example is the headrest ⵣ, an important piece of furniture
in Ancient Egyptian households and burial equipment. Its pictorial representation exists among the hieroglyphic sign repertoire and was used as a determinative (more specifically: repeater) of *wrs* 'headrest', although the generic sign ⌒
for wood and woodwork could also be used in hieroglyphic within the same
word. Hieratic uses of repeaters and other very specific graphs were much more
infrequent than their hieroglyphic counterparts, and whenever the word *wrs*
'headrest' makes its appearance in hieratic inventories of household and tomb
furniture, the determinative ⌒ is used consistently (Haring 2018: 32). The
differences in uses of signs by scribes of monumental and cursive texts require
more research and may throw important light on determinatives as reflections of
semantic categories as well as scribal conventions and innovations.

## 2.2 Phonographic Writing: Consonants and Syllables

Ancient Egyptian phonographic writing was essentially consonantal, but orthographic strategies existed to indicate the presence and quality of vowels –
although never sufficient to reconstruct ancient pronunciation. Since the same
hieroglyphic signs and orthographies were used for thousands of years, during
which the Egyptian language changed considerably, their reference to actual
sounds, and their understanding as such by modern readers, can only be
approximations (see e.g. Loprieno 1995: 28). The sound represented by
𓅐 (the Egyptian vulture), for instance, is thought to have been /r/ or /l/ in the
earliest documented stages of the language, but /ʔ/ (glottal stop, *'aleph*) in later

---

[18] For instance, two detailed renderings of craftsmen's instruments (level and plumb rule) as
determinatives in Siut tombs I and IV (sketchily drawn in Griffith 1889: pl. 6, col. 265; pl. 13,
col. 32; precise forms in Kahl & Shafik 2021: 246–7, nos. U39H and U97; for the former, see also
Haring 2018: 222–3) are two rare signs whose use may have been prompted by the equally rare
words they follow.

[19] There are examples of very specific and detailed determinatives in hieratic, such as the occa-
sional use of the horse 𓄛 (reversed for unknown reasons) as determinative of *ḥtr* 'chariot-span'
in a manuscript that otherwise uses the generic 'animal' determinative 𓃗 (P. Sallier III col. 1, lines
6 and 9: Kitchen 1979: 29 and 31; Budge 1923: pl. LXXVII – note the sketches of horses in the
upper margin of the manuscript, as exercises?). Hieratic scribes frequently chose to abbreviate
complex signs to a diagonal stroke, but were not always averse to adding an elaborate determinative – for example, in *ḥḏt* 'white crown' in P. Chester Beatty I verso B 19: ⟍𓋑 (with stroke
and the actual crown); recto col. 16, line 1: 𓋔𓋑 (mistakenly with the double crown), recto col.
8, line 4: 𓃂𓋑 with the generic determinative for divinity instead of a crown, highlighting the
divine qualities of the king and his attributes. The last determinative looks very simple in its
cursive form. Hieratic originals can be found in Gardiner 1931: pl. VIII, XVI, XX. Like
hieroglyphs, cursive scripts sometimes insert more or less detailed pictograms on the same
scale as the surrounding signs, functioning as ad hoc logograms, the phonetic rendering of which
often escapes us (examples in Polis & Rosmorduc 2015: 159–61).

periods (Loprieno 1995: 15). For some signs, it is entirely uncertain which sounds of the Egyptian language they are supposed to represent. A case in point is ⟨, a stylized rendering of a flowering reed. Read as /i/ by Champollion (who assumed that the hieroglyphic script included a set of vowel signs), it was later thought to represent a consonant that could be either /j/ (*yod*), or /ʔ/, these two consonants possibly being again the earlier and the later sounds rendered by the sign. Several current Egyptological transliteration systems use *j*. The sign has also been argued to have represented a vowel onset or a glottal stop from its earliest appearance, and as such, an indication of vowel presence (Peust 2016). One consequence of that argument is that /j/ is not represented by any mono-consonantal sign in hieroglyphic,[20] a circumstance Peust explained as due to the fact that the initial /j/ was absent in older Egyptian (Peust 2016: 95). This explanation implies that word-initial occurrence of sounds was decisive for their being separately encoded in hieroglyphic and, by inference, that acrophony was important for the perception of sounds as separate phonetic units to be rendered in writing. This is an important point, to which we will return.

Non-initial /j/ must have been frequent in spoken Egyptian, and one way to indicate it was the *pair* of flowering reeds ⟨⟨, as becomes clear from Ancient Egyptian transcriptions of foreign words containing *yod*, such as 𓀀𓂝𓏤𓏭 *mryn* '(chariot) warrior', *maryanu* in cuneiform Ugaritic (Hoch 1994: 135–7; see Section 5.2). In foreign loanwords, even the initial /j/ seems to be indicated by ⟨⟨, for instance in 𓈖𓏭 *ym* 'sea' (cf. Biblical Hebrew *yam* 'sea'; Hoch 1994: 52–3).[21] Both *ym* and *mryn* are instances of so-called group or syllabic writing, in which individual consonants are expressed by pairs or even more elaborate groups of hieroglyphic signs (thus ⟨⟨ or ₉⟨⟨ for *y*). This notation was mainly, but not exclusively, used for the transcription of foreign words in Egyptian.[22] Many Egyptologists assume that it renders consonants together with vowels, although opinions differ on how exactly the supposed 'syllabic' groups of hieroglyphs would do that (see mainly Hoch 1994: 487–512; Kilani 2019). The use of ⟨⟨ was by no means restricted to group writing. It was frequently used at the end of words, and is thought to indicate word-final /j/ or a glide before a word-final vowel (e.g. Allen 2020: 145–60). In Old and Middle Egyptian, for instance, important classes of verbal roots ending in whatever sound

---

[20] I prefer 'mono-consonantal', 'biconsonantal' and so forth over 'uniliteral', 'biliteral' and so forth (the latter being current in grammars of Ancient Egyptian), since the signs are supposed to represent sounds (consonants). Words like 'uniliteral' are appropriate only in the context of transliteration – that is, the rendering of hieroglyphic signs visually by means of our *letters*.

[21] This is commonly assumed by Egyptologists. Peust (2016: 94–5) expressed doubts about ⟨⟨ representing initial /j/, and suggested bi-syllabic *i-am* 'sea'.

[22] Group writing is best known from Late Egyptian orthography, but the practice is already attested in the Old Kingdom; see Hoch 1994: 487 ff.; Edel 1955–64: 21–2.

was expressed by ⏀ (usually not written, hence called 'weak') in certain verb forms ended with ⏀⏀, as when their 'weak' final consonant combined with the ending *-w* of passive verbal inflexions (Edel 1955–64: 240–1; Allen 2014: 290; e.g. ⟨ᴐ *jr(j)* 'to make' > passive 𝟫⟨ᴐ *jr(j)w* or ⏀⏀⟨ᴐ *jry* 'made'). In Late Egyptian (which was not common as a written language before *c.*1300 BC), the signs ⏀⏀ and // may reflect the endings of 'weak' verbs (Winand 1992: 100; cf. Schenkel 1994: 12–14) and of feminine nouns that have dropped their 'weak' ending ⊃ *t* (Junge 2008: 34). In the ever-archaic hieroglyphic orthography, the sign ⊃, in spite of having lost its phonetic significance, is often retained together with ⏀⏀. These examples must suffice here to illustrate the reflection of Ancient Egyptian vocalization in hieroglyphic orthography, which is tantalizing but never sufficient to reconstruct actual pronunciation.[23]

## 2.3 Consonants, *Abjad*s and Acrophony

Egyptian hieroglyphic writing has been labelled 'syllabic' in comparative research in the past, but this is no longer accepted; both Egyptologists and scholars of other fields adhere to the view that Pharaonic Egyptian writing was basically consonantal.[24] Comparative linguist Peter Daniels (2018: 113) refers to Egyptian hieroglyphs as 'morphoconsonantal' – that is, a combination of 'morphographic' and consonantal writing. This he contrasts with logosyllabic writing, in which syllabic signs originated from logograms for monosyllabic words, as evidenced by, for example, Sumerian, Chinese, and Maya. Syllables, rather than individual sounds or phonemes, are widely considered the natural way in which speakers break up their languages into discrete phonetic units.[25] Daniels' contention is that original grammatogenies – that is, writing systems developed without the presence or knowledge of pre-existing ones – can only be

---

[23] Reconstruction is possible to a limited extent, and mainly in diachronic perspective, as the examples here demonstrate. Synchronic reconstruction (i.e. the reconstruction of Egyptian vocalization at any point of its history) remains elusive (Loprieno 1995: 28 ff.). For an elaborate discussion of Egyptian historical phonology, focusing on the later language stages (Late Egyptian–Coptic), see Peust 1999.

[24] Gelb (1952: 76–81) admitted that the *quality* of the vowels in the supposed syllables is not specified by hieroglyphs – which basically invalidates the argument. Gelb proceeded from the unlikelihood, in his opinion, that logographic writing could develop directly into consonantal notation, without the syllabary as an intermediate stage. He stated that Old Hebrew and related scripts are syllabic too (Gelb 1952: 166 ff.), but see Daniels 2018: 133–5.

[25] See the foreword by the cognitive scientist David Share in Daniels (2018), mentioning 'the ready psychological accessibility of the syllable (as opposed to the phoneme)' (xi). A similar observation, with non-literate speakers specifically, is made by the anthropologist Alfred Kroeber (136). Andrew Davidson (2019) argues that phonemes, words and sentences, although real entities in spoken language, are 'constructed' in the speakers' brains by writing. He refers to the results of various cognitive researchers demonstrating that 'alphabetic literacy enhances discrimination at a sub-syllabic level, at the level of what is represented by the grapheme' (144).

syllabaries (Daniels 2018: 84). The obvious consequence for Egyptian hiero-glyphs would be that they do not represent an original grammatogeny, but were developed under the influence of an already existing writing system, Sumerian (Daniels 2018: 141–2). Contact, direct or indirect, between Egypt and Mesopotamia in the Pre- and Early Dynastic Period is clearly evidenced by shared aspects of material culture, such as cylinder seals (see Section 5.1), imagery on prestige items and monumental mudbrick architecture featuring decorative clay cones and recess façades. Shared features in the development of writing, which took place in both regions in approximately the same period, are to be expected. Mesopotamian inspiration for the development of writing in Egypt has often been considered, but the exact nature of the cultural and language contact between the two regions, and its possible influence on script development, remains obscure. There is no evidence of Mesopotamian phonetic writing being used significantly earlier than its Egyptian counterpart. What is more, nothing hints at specific Mesopotamian ways of phonetic notation as the source of early Egyptian phoneticism. In a recent analysis, Andréas Stauder emphasizes the differences between early phonetic notations in both regions, arguing that Egyptian phoneticism developed entirely within the context of regional visual culture (Stauder 2022: 253–71), and that modes of phonetic writing do not depend on the type of language (273). The development of Egypt's specific strategy of phonetic writing may thus have been independent from external impulses, perhaps with the exception of a shared idea of visually rendering linguistic utterances. Ludwig Morenz suspected that an important stimulus for the development of phonetic writing in Egypt was precisely the presence of foreign (i.e. North African and Near Eastern) languages, inviting ways to write words that had no meaning in Egyptian – a process in a way comparable to the later development of the 'syllabic' orthography discussed earlier in this Element (Morenz 2004: 228–34).

Mesopotamian pictorial (subsequently cuneiform) characters stood for syl-lables – that is, clusters of consonants and vowels – which remained unchanged in the linguistic structure of Sumerian. By contrast, Egyptian and Semitic languages work with consonantal skeletons and variable patterns of vocaliza-tion. This linguistic feature may have been of some importance to the develop-ment of consonantal writing in Egypt and the Near East. Whereas Mesopotamian inspiration in the development of Egyptian consonantal writing is uncertain, it seems likely that the latter did inspire the earliest consonantal writing of West-Semitic (as sketched briefly in Daniels 2018: 142–3). We will return to that particular process in Section 5.3, but mention should be made here already of Semitic consonantal 'alphabets', or *abjad*s, as they are more appro-priately called. Whereas alphabets, in the strictest definition, include vowel signs (such as the Greek and later European alphabets), *abjad*s (or *abgad*s) are their consonantal counterparts, even their precursors. The Greek *alpha-beta-gamma-delta* (α-β-γ-δ) goes back to a West-Semitic *'aleph-bet-gimel-dalet* (in Biblical Hebrew vocalisation, for *'-b-g-d*, hence *'abgad*). Both alphabets and *abjad*s are approximations of the sets of distinctive sounds (phonemes) in the languages they encode – although *abjad*s concentrate on consonants. That is, these scripts are based on a division of spoken language in segments or sounds, not syllables. Viewed by linguists and anthropologists as secondary with respect to syllabic scripts in the historical development of writing systems, such 'phonemic' systems may indeed betray a re-conceptualization of spoken language by their inventors. Their analysis may even have been influenced by the very existence of writing, since literate speakers are more capable of segmenting their language in individual sounds than illiterates (Daniels 2018: 158–9; Davidson 2019).

In addition to their phonemic segmentation, alphabets and *abjad*s are scripts with fixed and very limited sets of characters, since these render individual sounds only, not combinations of them, and include no ideograms. The Hebrew *abjad* has twenty-two characters, the classical Greek alphabet has twenty-four, and the English alphabet has twenty-six. Hieroglyphic Egyptian remains the earliest known writing system that breaks language down into phonemes, but conventional Egyptian phonographic writing was never detached from the ideographic qualities of the same script (logo- or radicograms and determinatives). Yet it is significant that Egyptian phonograms include signs that express single consonants (twenty-four different consonants were distinguished in Old and Middle Egyptian). These are commonly found as phonetic complements, such as 𓄿 *m* in ___𓄿𓈖 *sḏm* (see Section 2.1), but they were also used without logograms in mono-consonantal orthography, especially in the earliest written Egyptian (Early Dynastic and Old Kingdom, *c*.2900–2100 BC). Thus, Old Kingdom hieroglyphic texts could write *sḏm* as 𓄿𓈖𓏤 or 𓈖𓄿𓂋𓏤, spelled out with individual consonants as *s-ḏ-m*. In the first example, a very frequent spelling, a determinative is absent, presumably because the ear logogram was deemed sufficiently informative, while in the second example, the absence of that logogram necessitates the use of a more specific determinative – the ear instead of the otherwise frequently used papyrus scroll. Two-thirds of the sign occurrences in the extensive corpus of Old Kingdom Pyramid Texts are those of mono-consonantal signs, and the corpus even includes sections written in these signs only (Kammerzell 2001: 123–5; see also Schweitzer 2003: 375–7, 379–85). In the absence of logograms and determinatives, this makes them very difficult to decipher. A recent case study on the Old Kingdom writings of the word *rmṯ* 'people' by Ibrahim

Abd El-Sattar is revealing in this respect. The oldest preserved versions of the Pyramid Texts (in the pyramids of Unas and Teti, around 2300 BC) prefer the bare phonetic writing �⌡ *r-m-ṯ*, without logograms or determinatives. Some Teti versions have the plural determinative ° ° °; the slightly later texts of Pepi I have either these or plural strokes. It is only from his successor Merenre onward that we find human figures as determinatives, although 'mutilated' in the sense that only the arms, shoulders and heads of men and women are shown, not the full figures (Abd El-Sattar 2021: 1–2). The reluctance to represent full human figures, or even human figures at all, is certainly a characteristic of these royal funerary texts as a genre. From the early Old Kingdom onward, royal decrees and private funerary texts preferred spellings with logograms or determinatives, the most frequent writings being ⌈glyphs⌉ (phonetic writing *r(-m-)ṯ* with determinatives) and ⌈glyphs⌉ (logograms only; Abd El-Sattar 2021: 2–6).[26]

'Phonemic awareness' by the producers of hieroglyphs and hieratic can also be deduced from the practice of abbreviating words and names to single hieroglyphs. This is frequently done in regular hieroglyphic writing, both with logograms or radicograms (e.g. ⌈glyph⌉ as bare logographic writing of *sḏm*, or ⌈glyph⌉ for *ʿnḫ* 'to live'), and with phonograms (e.g. simple prepositions like ⌈glyph⌉ *m* 'in' and ⌈glyph⌉ *r* 'to', which are obviously consonantal reductions of the vocalized words as pronounced).[27] Hieroglyphic abbreviations are also found outside texts, as emblems and marks, which will be addressed in Sections 3.1 and 4.2. Texts may include individual signs that are not part of written phrases or sentences; sometimes even lists of such signs. The lists of an administrative hieratic text from the reign of Senusert I (Papyrus Reisner II, *c.*1900 BC) incorporate non-hieratic signs, which refer to teams of workmen or the places they came from. They are thus to be regarded as identity marks, such as are also found in non-textual contexts, functioning, for instance, as property marks on tools (Andrássy 2009b). At least some of these marks are hieroglyphic abbreviations of top-onyms (e.g. ⌈glyph⌉ for *Nbyt* 'Ombos'; Andrássy 2009b: 118). A list of similarly abbreviated toponyms is found in one of the rare lexical lists that have survived from pharaonic Egypt, the so-called Ramesseum Onomasticon. One section of this text is a list of toponyms in hieratic, each name accompanied by a single

---

[26] A more extended version of this spelling with plural strokes ⌈glyphs⌉, attested from the Sixth Dynasty onward, would remain the classical spelling for centuries (Abd El-Sattar 2021: 4). Interestingly, the *m* omitted in writing was maintained in the spoken language throughout Egyptian history while *ṯ* disappeared; compare Coptic *rōme*. Such omissions of word-internal consonants are connected with the syllabic structure of words in spoken Egyptian by Kahl (1992).

[27] Indeed, they are abbreviations of fuller, 'vocalized' spellings ⌈glyph⌉ and ⌈glyph⌉, both with ⌈glyph⌉ as *Anlaut*, the former only in pronominal forms (i.e. with suffix pronouns) or as an adverb, the latter also before nouns (in Old and Middle Egyptian: Edel 1955–64: 388–91; Allen 2014: 106–7).

sign in hieratic or hieroglyphic, which serves as an abbreviation (Gardiner 1947: 11–13, pl. II). Among them is ⌐⌐⌐ for *Nbyt* 'Ombos'. Especially interesting are three toponyms starting with *jwn*: *Jwnyt* 'Esna', *Jwny* 'Armant' and *Jwnt* 'Dendera'. The obvious sign presenting itself as an abbreviation in all three cases would be the pillar ⌐ as radicogram for *jwn*, but since a distinction between the three places had to be made, this single sign was chosen to denote *Jwnyt* 'Esna' only; the same sign but with phonetic complement ⌐ (*jwn* + *n*) denoted *Jwny* 'Armant' and, perhaps surprisingly, ⌐⌐⌐ (*n*) alone denoted *Jwnt* 'Dendera'. Although phonetics may have played a role in the choice for the last example, that choice may have been the logical consequence of the selections made for the previous two abbreviations, since ⌐ and ⌐⌐⌐ are the only two signs that appear in the full orthographies of all three toponyms. In another case, the actual pronunciation of a place name must have been the reason for the abbreviation chosen: the sign ⌐ *d* to denote ⌐⌐⌐⌐ *Ḏbꜣ* 'Edfu'. Although the radicogram ⌐ *ḏbꜣ*, the first sign of the full writing, presented itself as a very characteristic visual abbreviation, the choice was made to use a sign that did not even occur in the name as spelled out in hieratic. Therefore, it must have been a *phonetic* abbreviation, the more so since the initial *ḏ* represents a sound that, in many words, had actually evolved to *d*, as had taken place in the name 'Edfu' by the time the Ramesseum Onomasticon was written. On the basis of this particular abbreviation, Alan Gardiner (1947: 12) credited the scribe of the onomasticon with 'a consciousness of the alphabet', something we will return to in Section 5.3 and in the Conclusion.

Phonetic reductions, such as the ones discussed in the previous paragraphs, bring us back to the subject of acrophony, already briefly touched upon in Section 2.2. Acrophony is the reduction of a linguistic utterance (a word or phrase) to its initial sound. The continuous stream of sound that is a word or a longer utterance is open to different ways of division into phonetic units (such as the syllables and phonemes discussed previously), but the very first sound of that utterance is clear, whatever division strategy is followed. For this reason, word-initial sounds as perceived would have played a crucial role in the development of phonographic writing, and more particularly in phonemic writing. The Egyptian mono-consonantal signs are a case in point. Many, if not all, of these signs appear to be reductions of short (monosyllabic) words, as is clearly outlined by Pascal Vernus (2015: 151–8). These included words with the 'weak' feminine ending *t*, which was dropped in pronunciation, such as the noun *ḫt* 'belly', written with an animal's belly ⌐ as a logogram, or more fully ⌐ which through phonetic reduction resulted in *ḫ* + vowel, and hence became a phonogram ⌐ for *ḫ* in the hieroglyphic writing system. Or they could be words ending in a 'weak' consonant such as ⌐⌐⌐ *qꜣ* 'height'/'hill'(?), featuring the hillside ⌂ that became a phonogram for $q$ (155). This was probably how the mono-consonantal set of signs in Egypt's earliest hieroglyphic writing came into being, but even more such signs would be developed by the same processes during the course of its history (157–8). Similar processes are at the basis of the 'syllabic' group writing mentioned previously; in that particular case, vowels are thought to be implied by groups of signs (e.g. 𓄿 ⌂ for $q$ + vowel), as opposed to single signs representing single consonants alone.

Such processes of reduction, based on developments in the spoken language, are called 'weak' acrophony by Vernus, and contrasted by him with 'strong' acrophony, in which more than one consonant following the initial one, regardless of their 'weak' or 'strong' nature, are left out (160). The example of ⟟ $d$ for *Ḏbꜣ* 'Edfu' in the previous paragraph is a clear case of 'strong' acrophony. It is perhaps better to introduce here the word 'acrography', since it is the *graphic* result of the *linguistic* reduction process that is of principal interest to us, and because it seems unlikely that *Ḏbꜣ*/'Edfu' was really abbreviated to a mere consonant /d/ in the spoken language.[28] Rather than a natural linguistic process like weak acrophony, strong acrophony (or acrography) is a conscious choice on the part of speakers, and especially on the part of inventors and users of writing and of other graphic notations. It plays a vital role in the development of enigmatic hieroglyphic writing (Section 3.2) and new scripts inspired by hieroglyphs (Sections 5.2–3).

## 3 Putting Up Barriers: Hyper-Specialist Writing

### 3.1 Monumental Writing–Image Interchange: Emblematic Hieroglyphs

The hieroglyphic script was designed for monumental display from the start. The proto-hieroglyphs on pottery vessels and on tags of bone, ivory and wood from a royal tomb inventory of the late fourth millennium (see Section 2) can be argued to have served as a display during the burial rites, and the sustained expression of identity and power after closure of the tomb. Early hieroglyphs complement other types of imagery on votive palettes, maceheads, seals and tags. Combinations of picture and writing set the pattern for Egyptian art from tomb and temple walls and monumental sculpture, to small decorated objects, for millennia. By their pictorial nature, hieroglyphs may appear as components which are fully integrated in a visual composition, such as a monumental scene carved or painted on a wall of a tomb or a temple, especially when they have been delicately made with carved or painted details. Very often, hieroglyphs

---

[28] Compare the notation 'LA', a *graphic* abbreviation of 'Los Angeles', *pronounced* 'el-ay'.

**Figure 3** Thutmose IV depicted in his colonnaded chapel, Karnak. Photo by the author.

were added to such compositions in vertical columns or horizontal lines separated from the scene and from each other by framing lines, so that text and image were kept separate. But individual signs or small clusters of them could also be added without framing at various places in the scene, usually directly over or beside the figures they related to (e.g. when rendering personal names or titles, or a conversation between two human figures). They could even be images in their own right. For instance, hieroglyphs could be 'anthropomorphized' by giving them human arms, making them capable of holding attributes and performing actions. Among the symbols depicted behind the king in ritual scenes may be hieroglyphs for *ankh* 'life' ☥ and *djed* 'stability' with human arms holding fans and other attributes (Figure 3). A more complex example can be seen on tags and seal impressions of one of the earliest Egyptian kings, featuring his name, Aha (ꜥḥꜣ) 'Warrior' written with a single radicogram representing human arms with a mace (or an axe) and shield (Figure 4).[29] This was the king's 'Horus name' – that is, the name he bore as the incarnation of the sky god Horus. It was usual to have this name written inside a palace façade with the falcon representing Horus (i.e. the king) on top. We are actually looking at three hieroglyphs (falcon, façade, Aha) combined in such a way that

---

[29] The hieroglyphic type here is based on much later forms of the sign; see Gardiner 1957: 453, no. D 34.

**Figure 4** Seal impression mentioning King Aha. From Kaplony 1963: pl. 29, no. 79; reproduced here with kind permission of the publisher.

the arms holding weapon and shield are actually extensions of the falcon's talons through the top of the palace. By means of these extensions the three signs are merged; the king/falcon is holding his weapons and indeed his name. Such playful extensions and combinations of hieroglyphic signs have been labelled 'emblematic uses' by John Baines, a mode 'between representation and writing' (Baines 2007: 285).

Equally playful are hieroglyphs as constituent parts of a figure by way of a rebus expressing that figure's identity. A clear example, and one well known to Egyptologists, is the figure of the deity Re, the sun, in the façade of the rock temple of Ramesses II (1279–1216 BC) at Abu Simbel. Re is depicted in high relief, with a human body and the head of a falcon, and crowned with the sun disc. Although the figure is slightly damaged, two attributes beside its lower legs can still be recognized as 𓌀 *wsr* 'force' and 𓐙 *Mꜣꜥt*, the personified Truth. What appeared at first to be a depiction of the sun god now turns out to be a rebus for *Wsr-Mꜣꜥt-Rꜥ* 'Userma'atre', the throne name of Ramesses II, who equated himself to the sun god on more than one monument.[30]

In such compositions, the pictorial nature of hieroglyphs is exploited to the fullest. Pharaonic culture was not alone in doing so. Other cultures with pictorial scripts provide comparable examples. Maya hieroglyphs can be incorporated in visual compositions in ways very similar to Egyptian ones. One stela at Seibal,

---

[30] See also other examples among statuary of Ramesses II who, although certainly not the only king to have left such three-dimensional text–image interaction, appears to have had a particular taste for it (Laboury 2022a: 152–3; Pietri 2022: 155–6).

Guatemala, depicts the Maya ruler B'ot (*c*.800 CE) flanked by columns of hieroglyphs, which are thus easily recognized as writing, and to be viewed separately from the central image of the king, although related to it. But the king is also standing on a hieroglyphic group that says 'Six Stair Place'. This is the name of the place for the performance of the ritual Maya ball game, in which the king is on the point of engaging (Boot 2005: 62–3).[31] Chinese and Japanese calligraphic compositions may also use the iconicity of signs (although their iconicity is less explicit than that of Egyptian and Maya hieroglyphs) to combine visual and linguistic expression (see examples in Elkins 1999: 114–17).

Scholars advocate that, even in visual compositions involving highly pictorial writing, text remains text and image remains image. On the basis of examples in Turkish and Japanese calligraphy, the art historian James Elkins concluded that 'Picture and writing are very close, but worlds apart' (Elkins 1999: 103). Egyptologist John Baines stated with respect to Early Dynastic inscribed objects: 'Even though there is relatively little stylistic disjunction between representation and writing, direct interplay between the two media, in which figures act as hieroglyphs or hieroglyphs as figures …, is less common than is sometimes implied: conventions of scale and other details almost always keep the two separate, and no one confuses picture with script' (Baines 2007: 285).[32] In later periods, examples of direct interplay, such as the image of Re on the Abu Simbel façade, abound and demonstrate that pharaonic art could achieve a relatively complete merger of image and text. One may object that it is difficult, if not impossible, to see the same object at the same time as image and as writing and that, as soon as the literate mind discovers the Userma'atre rebus on the Abu Simbel façade, the image is reduced to text. But the colossal image itself is too prominent for that. One may also disagree that the visual (even three-dimensional) expression of a name or epithet is not that much of a linguistic message; hence, it is not real 'text'. But text it is, however brief.

An important point to consider here is the knowledge of the spectator, more precisely, the viewer's literate skills and familiarity with visual expression. Baines observed that in early Egypt, both text and artistic expression were seen by a narrow elite only: 'Those who used representation also used writing', to which he adds,

---

[31] More parallels with Mesoamerica are referred to by Baines (2007: 281) and Houston and Stauder (2020).

[32] The opposition between image and writing and their integration are persistent topics in semiotic research. Roy Harris has noted how modes of visual communication other than writing are usually defined by their being different from it (Harris 1986: 131; compare notions like 'non-textual', 'non-verbal'). In Harris' integrative semiology, the term 'writing' is extended to different forms of visual communication, with distinction made between 'glottic' and 'non-glottic' writing (Harris 1995: 94). The latter category includes sign systems of single and double articulation; those of single articulation (see Section 2.1) were called 'emblems' by Harris; this is a notion different from that of 'emblematic use' of signs in the current section as advocated by John Baines.

**Figure 5** Lintel of Senusert III, Karnak. Photo by the author.

interestingly, that access to representations was probably even more limited than literacy (Baines 2007: 291).[33] With the increase of monumental display in later Egyptian history, artistic expression may have come to the attention of larger groups of the population, although access to temples and monumental tombs (places of artistic and hieroglyphic display par excellence) was always restricted. That the colossal statues of human figures wearing crowns were representations of kings would have been obvious to many, but decoding the intricate combination of text and image on a stela or a temple wall required hieroglyphic *and* iconographic knowledge. Particularly complex examples are elaborately inscribed lintels of temple doorways from the Middle Kingdom (Figure 5). It takes very specific literate and iconographic skills to understand the meaning of such compositions, and precisely what in them is picture and what is writing. To the illiterate observer, all would be picture, and without the knowledge to decode the picture, its precise meaning would remain obscure. We touch here on two different sorts of literacy: linguistic literacy (i.e. literacy in the traditional sense) and visual (or iconic) literacy (Elkins 1999: 23, 212; Haring 2018: 101). The latter term refers to the ability to decode visual representations without the presence or intercession of writing (e.g. as in prehistoric art; e.g. Perego 2013). Although only the fully literate (in the visual and linguistic sense) would have been able to sufficiently decode and disentangle a piece of sculpture or a painted scene with hieroglyphic inscriptions, those less knowledgeable would merely have recognized some elements of such compositions and connected them with notions familiar to them. Since Egyptian signs (whether hieroglyphs or purely pictorial elements) usually allowed more than one restricted reading, spectators could assign different values to signs when concentrating on them individually.[34]

---

[33] Literacy would extend, of course, to users of cursive scripts, outside the domain of monumental art.

[34] As is eloquently illustrated by Dimitri Laboury regarding the sign of the sun ⊙, which could be taken to mean the sun as such, the solar deity Re in any of his capacities, or the notion of 'day' (*hrw*: Laboury 2022a: 146). Note that through its meaning of 'day', the sign could even represent

Only the literate in both senses were able to disentangle the combined complexities of picture and hieroglyphic writing, and it is likely – even after the Early Dynastic Period – that the group fully cognisant of the relevant visual codes was even smaller than the linguistically literate part of the population. The core of that small group would have been the creators of two- and three-dimensional artistic objects and their hieroglyphic inscriptions, the so-called draughtsmen (*sš-qdw*, literally 'contour painter/scribes'). This Egyptological translation is conventional but misleading, as it suggests that the bearers of the title merely had the technical abilities to execute a painting or sculpture, once composed by more artistic or intellectual specialists. But these 'draughtsmen' were precisely the artists and intellectuals capable of composing monumental depictions and hieroglyphic inscriptions, as has been effectively illustrated in Egyptology by Dimitri Laboury (2013, 2020, 2022a, 2022b). The production of two- and three-dimensional art, and the drafting of hieroglyphic texts were thus in the hands of the same *artiste savant et lettré* (Laboury 2022a: 153). Although rejecting a polarized distinction between Egyptian writing and iconography, and regarding the border between them as permeable, Laboury also observes that the difference is generally obvious (2022a: 150: 'la separation entre écriture et iconographie est dans la pratique assez évidente'). This is true in cases where text can be distinguished from accompanying images by its typography (in lines or columns, with all signs or sign groups of equal size), but a more intricate entanglement of image and writing potentially reduces the accessibility of an entire composition for those less knowledgeable. As a consequence, the gap between (linguistically and visually) fully literate and the less literate became wider. It would become wider still through the development of more pictorial and otherwise playful writing in later phases of Egyptian history, which will be briefly discussed in Section 3.2.

## 3.2 Enigmatic and Ptolemaic Writing

The intricate combinations of images and hieroglyphic texts discussed in Section 3.1 were the work of highly accomplished specialists and so, of course, was the creation of hieroglyphic texts themselves. Play within hieroglyphic texts could be taken further still, beyond the usual graphic repertoire, and beyond the usual combinations of ideograms and phonograms. Playful writing may occur, and does occur, in many a hieroglyphic text. Common orthographic diversity (see Section 2) already indicates the potential for a high degree of

---

other Egyptian words – for example, *r* or *sw*. As a determinative, it could be used with a wide range of words to do with time – for example, 'hour', 'month', 'year', 'age/period', 'lifetime', 'eternity'.

versatility. Two particular applications of the script, however, consistently pushed hieroglyphic orthography to extremes, and the two are certainly related. One is the so-called enigmatic writing, while the other is Ptolemaic writing. The latter's name suggests that its use was restricted to the Ptolemaic Period (332–31 BC), but it actually continued to be employed into the Roman Period, and built on intricate hieroglyphic orthographies of pre-Ptolemaic times. Such earlier uses, referred to as 'enigmatic', range between isolated special signs or clusters of signs in otherwise regular hieroglyphic inscriptions, to fully enigmatic texts. The last are particularly well known in, but certainly not restricted to, royal tombs of the New Kingdom. The incidental insertion of graphical and orthographic playfulness already starts infrequently in the Old Kingdom (Darnell 2020: 7), but it is not until the New Kingdom that we find fully enigmatic texts in tombs and temples, and on private statues.

The strategies of enigmatic texts include on the level of (a) the individual sign: the substitution of one sign for another, and the creation of new signs, and (b) sign combinations: the reduction of usual combinations of ideograms and phonograms to phonetic writings in the form of single consonants exclusively. Single sign substitution may have different grounds for use, such as association, graphic similarity, meronymy and acrophony (for an overview, see Stauder 2020; Werning 2022). Full enigmatic orthography involves more than one of these strategies. Substitution of ideograms and phonograms is typical; examples include ⋈ (the symbol of the goddess *Nt* 'Neith') for *n* (normally spelled ～ or 𓈖), a mono-consonantal sign obtained by acrophonic reduction, and the star ★ instead of the usual ⌂ (sun rising over a hill), for *ḥꜥ* 'to appear', being an example of associative substitution. Reduction of entire texts to mono-consonantal orthography is characteristic of religious texts in the royal tombs of the New Kingdom in the Valley of the Kings. The sequence 𓏥𓏤 𓈖 𓈖 𓈖 𓈖, for instance, is found several times introducing a group of deities depicted on the second of four gilded shrines which enclosed the sarcophagus of Tutankhamen discovered in that king's tomb (Stauder 2020: 261–2). It reads: *n-n-n-n-ṯ-r*-[plural], for *nn n nṯr(w)* 'these gods … '. Determinatives are relatively rare in this type of notation; here and elsewhere the strokes I I I have been maintained as determinative of the plural. 'God' (*nṯr*) would normally be spelled with the logogram 𓊹, sometimes extended with a stroke determinative I, while phonetic complements ⌓ (*t-r*) would be used in *nṯr*-based derivations, such as *nṯrt* 'goddess' or *nṯry* 'divine'. The plural 'gods' (*nṯrw*) was normally spelled 𓊹𓊹𓊹. Thus the enigmatic writing 𓏥𓈖 was totally different from the spelling of *nṯrw* in regular hieroglyphic, as was the preceding 𓈖𓈖𓈖 for *nn n* 'these', which is normally written ～𓏌𓏌 (*nn-n-n*). Not only was regular hieroglyphic orthography reduced to signs for single consonants, many of the signs themselves were also substituted for the usual ones. Whereas 〔glyph〕 and 〔glyph〕 were common for *n* and *t* in regular hieroglyphic writing (although ⚊ and ⌒ were more frequent), 〔glyph〕 was actually the biconsonantal *rw*. Since the second consonant in that group was a 'weak' one (*w*), use of the recumbent lion for *r* would seem to be a case of 'weak' acrophony;[35] the same sign was supposedly used for *r* + vowel in 'syllabic' writing (see Section 2.3). But phonetic derivation by acrophony was not the only principle at work in enigmatic substitution; association, graphic similarity, and meronymy have already been mentioned earlier in this section. Graphic similarity or semantic association led to the use of the duck sign 〔glyph〕, a generic determinative for birds in regular hieroglyphic spelling, as a substitute for other bird signs, such as mono-consonantal 〔glyph〕 (*ꜣ*), 〔glyph〕 (*w*), 〔glyph〕 (*m*) and, less frequently, biconsonantal signs as 〔glyph〕 (*bꜣ*) and 〔glyph〕 (*nḥ*) (Roberson 2020: 91–3). In the case of mono-consonantal writing, such enigmatic substitutions surprisingly resulted in the reduction of the number of signs used, rather than multiplication, so that a core set of thirteen signs was sufficient to express the entire consonantal 'alphabet' (Werning 2022: 203). With its emphasis on phonographic writing and a minimum of determinatives (Meeks 2021: 560), the hierarchy of logograms, phonograms and determinatives characteristic of regular hieroglyphic writing was reduced to a bare phonetic sequence. As a consequence, writing and reading enigmatic texts was not about scanning words but about reading, or rather deciphering sign by sign (Stauder 2020: 250, 261; Meeks 2021: 561).

An entirely different type of enigmatic writing was the expression of royal and divine names and epithets in the form of rows of human figures or animals, the precise appearance and attributes of which indicated the sounds or words they referred to. A well-known example is the frieze of Ramesses II on one of the architraves of his courtyard in the Luxor temple (Klotz 2020: 63 ff.), actually an enigmatic dedicatory inscription. The frieze presents a row of divine figures, each one of which stands for a particular sound, word or name. Thus, for instance, the god Khonsu (identified by the lunar disc on his head), who typically expresses the notion of divine child, is for *ms(j)* 'to give birth'. In his hands he holds the hieroglyphs 〔glyph〕 *s* and 〔glyph〕 *sw*. Together with the preceding figure of Re (with sun disc), this reads *Rꜥ-ms-sw* 'Ramesses', a name literally meaning 'It is Re who gave birth

---

[35] The importance of acrophony in enigmatic and Ptolemaic writing has been a topic of debate among specialists. Initially stated by Étienne Drioton to have been the leading principle in phonetic derivations, its role was later seen to be more limited, as argued by Herbert Fairman, and actually just one of the ways to reduce the phonetic value of multilateral signs to the strong consonants in the sequence originally represented (Thiers 2022: 55–6). For instance, *ḥw* could be reduced to *ḥ*, an apparent case of (weak) acrophony, but in other cases, the discarded consonants preceded the strong ones, as in, for example, *jb*, when reduced to *b*.

to him' (67–8). In enigmatic writings of the name of Ramesses VI in that king's tomb, a standing figure of a male child, characteristically with a finger held to his mouth, following a figure of the sun god Re crowned with a sun disc, would also read *R͗-ms(-sw)* 'Ramesses' (Werning 2022: 203–4). The verb *ms(j)* 'to give birth' would normally be written with a group of signs starting with radicogram 𓄟 for *ms*, but in enigmatic writing the deity Khonsu or the figure of a child could render the same word by association. The same rebus, with the child holding a finger to his mouth, is again used in a statue of Ramesses II as a child (Pietri 2022: 155–6). The principle of that three-dimensional rebus is very similar to the Abu Simbel figure of Re (see Section 3.1), which thus also reveals itself to be 'enigmatic'. A very late example, well known among Egyptologists, is the columns of ram and crocodile figures on the *pronaos* of the Esna temple, of the Roman Period, as expressions of hymns to the temple's main deity, Khnum. Crowns and other attributes of the animals and a limited number of accompanying hieroglyphs supposedly helped the ancient knowledgeable reader to decipher these long rebuses, but the hymns have baffled Egyptologists for a long time (Thiers 2022: 55; see Leitz 2001 for a detailed analysis).

Texts rendered as rows of deities and human figures in temples of the Ptolemaic and Roman Periods continued the tradition of enigmatic writing already found in the temples and royal tombs of the New Kingdom,[36] but hieroglyphic inscriptions in Ptolemaic temples also manifest a development that is typical for the period in which they were made: the multiplication of hieroglyphs (i.e. graphs) on the one hand, and the multiplication of meanings attached to each individual sign on the other. The number of possible phonetic values of individual signs, in particular, rose dramatically. The principles followed in assigning additional meanings to the hieroglyphs were the same as those in enigmatic sign substitutions, but did not result in a reduced set of phonograms.[37] On the contrary: Ptolemaic hieroglyphic writing, as the system is commonly called, is renowned for its thousands of graphic signs, with multiple meanings attached to each individual one.[38]

---

[36] In addition to the Khnum hymns mentioned in the previous paragraphs, see, for example, Cauville (1990, 2002).

[37] Ptolemaic phonograms include many different signs to express the same single consonants, as well as different mono-consonantal values of individual signs. Mono-consonantal hieroglyphic writing became popular from the seventh century BC onward; this has been considered an archaistic trend inspired by Old Kingdom examples. That assumption, as well as that of supposed inspiration by Greek alphabetic writing, has been refuted convincingly in recent studies; mono-consonantal orthography of this later period is more appropriately seen as one feature of the ongoing innovation of hieroglyphic writing that led to the intricate orthographic system of Ptolemaic writing (see Der Manuelian 1994: 81, 98–100, and especially Schweitzer 2003).

[38] Here as in the case of the 'classical' hieroglyphic script (see note 16), precise numbers are difficult to give. The number 7,000 often seen in Egyptological literature has justly been

Ptolemaic inscriptions represent the last stage in the development and active use of Egyptian hieroglyphs – the very last dated hieroglyphic inscription, presented in the Introduction, follows this particular writing system. In an increasingly Hellenizing Egypt, the application of this script was limited to the pharaonic temples that were the last strongholds of traditional Egyptian religion. This means that the composition of Ptolemaic hieroglyphic texts, and thus of hieroglyphic texts tout court, had become the exclusive domain of priests. Rather than employing the complicated script as a means to hide traditional religious texts from nosy Greek visitors, as has sometimes been assumed, the priests celebrated among themselves the antiquity of the texts, their depth of meaning, their graphic and associative play, and the perfect agreement with their specific architectural context (the latter aspect of Ptolemaic writing is demonstrated clearly in Leitz 2003).

That is, Ptolemaic writing was not meant to be 'cryptic' or 'secret', and neither was the enigmatic writing of earlier centuries, in spite of the adjective 'cryptic' still used for the latter sort of script. In both cases, for instance, the names, epithets and capacities of deities and kings may be rendered in extremely complicated ways at some places in a temple or tomb, but more easily readable (or 'regular' in the case of enigmatic texts) elsewhere in the same monument. The decoration of the second shrine of Tutankhamen is an example which combines enigmatic captions to the scenes with columns of regular hieroglyphic text. The term 'enigmatic' is appropriate in the sense that the reader's attention is required and his interest aroused by the complex uses and graphic manipulation of familiar hieroglyphs. The circle of the initiated, to be sure, was extremely limited. The use of an enigmatic script certainly defined a narrow group of high social and intellectual standing (Werning 2022: 205–6); Ptolemaic texts were produced by the most learned priests of their time, with temple schools playing an important role in the development of local hiero-glyphic particularities (Thiers 2022: 56–7). As Joachim Quack (2010: 241) put it, Ptolemaic was 'about conveying an added layer of meaning on the graphic level for a rather closed inner circle where social separation worked towards increased complexity of the system whose understanding became also a differ-entiating hallmark of an elite.'

That the use of enigmatic and Ptolemaic writing helped define a limited group of socially and intellectually privileged people can only be true, but what about the intended readership? The priestly specialists creating Ptolemaic temple texts

criticized by several specialists, since many 'signs' merely differ in graphic details while sharing the same meaning(s), and are hence not really different signs, but graphic variants of the same sign. The number of different signs is thought rather to be between 1,500 and 2,000 (Leitz 2009: 11; Quack 2010: 240–1) or between 2,000 and 2,500 (Thiers 2022: 54–5).

also frequented the immediate surroundings and inner spaces of the inscribed temples, but they were probably not the principal audience of the texts, many of which were located in high and pitch-dark sections of the inner rooms, or in subterranean crypts, and were therefore invisible to the human eye. This was even more true in the case of New Kingdom enigmatic texts in the royal tombs, which were off limits to mortals when closed after burial – and the innermost shrines surrounding Tutankhamen's sarcophagus would have been concealed from anyone except for their makers. Insofar as there *was* an intended readership, it must have been divine rather than human, and in that case consisted of deities and deceased pharaohs.[39]

This must also be true for statues erected in temples by private individuals, such as the one of Thutmose, deputy of the Egyptian governor of Nubia in the fourteenth century BC, who had a statue representing himself placed in an Egyptian temple in Semna, Nubia (now in the Museum of Fine Arts, Boston; Klotz & Brown 2016). The statue is covered with enigmatic hieroglyphic inscriptions, including the usual offering formula for his own benefit. Although donors of temple statues may have wished visitors to read and pronounce such offering formulas, who thus magically brought about the desired offerings, knowledgeable visitors must have been extremely scarce in faraway Semna. It may be true that Thutmose, a high Egyptian official with tasks that kept him abroad, 'felt compelled to boldly re-affirm his high Egyptian culture through this compelling and masterful self-representation', but the location of the statue was a difficult one for self-presentation to colleagues of his own standing (Klotz & Brown 2016: 300). We must assume, therefore, that Thutmose's intellectual self-definition did not so much address a circle of colleagues, but rather served as confirmation to the divine world and to himself (cf. Werning 2022: 206).

# 4 Limited Understanding and Creative Use of Hieroglyphs

## 4.1 Artists Less Accomplished

The previous sections have demonstrated that hieroglyphic writing, both in its 'regular' and even more challenging applications, was the specialization of a narrow group of artistic and priestly professionals. Their skills were the result of years of training and practice. One would perhaps expect that only fully trained and accomplished draughtsmen were allowed to work on the sculptures, reliefs and paintings in temples and tombs, but in fact, among the surviving monuments there are also many that betray the hands of less skillful or knowledgeable producers. Reference has already been made, in Section 2, to hieroglyphic

---

[39] Obviously the same was the case for many of the 'regular' hieroglyphic inscriptions.

**Figure 6** First Intermediate Period stela of Djari (Cairo JE 41437).
From Petrie (1909: pl. II).

inscriptions including (semi-)cursive signs, which indicate that their makers mastered cursive scripts but possessed limited hieroglyphic expertise. In actual cases of insufficient expertise, cursive or semi-cursive signs are not the only indicators: in such cases, also the style of the 'correct' hieroglyphs and of the entire hieroglyphic and visual compositions make clear that the work is not up to the highest quality standards.[40] The word 'insufficient' does not imply any absolute ancient standards. Producers and customers of private stelae in, for instance, a provincial town in the First Intermediate Period might very well have agreed on the quality of finished monuments as sufficient to their taste (Figure 6).[41]

The availability of high-quality craftsmanship, but also the very notion of what that would have meant, thus depended on the context – that is, the time and place in which monuments, their decorations and inscriptions were produced. But even at moments and locations in which high-quality craftsmanship was known to exist, getting access to it could be a challenge, even for the wealthy elite. As far as the extant pharaonic evidence allows us to say, fully accomplished artists were attached to the royal residence and to temples. Wealthy private individuals, usually members of the royal administration and the priesthood, as well as members of their families, could engage these artists only

---

[40] (Semi-)cursive signs or features could become permanent parts of the accepted monumental hieroglyphic repertoire once they had made their appearance in it. This is true for 'fully' cursive signs, usually abbreviations of more complex hieroglyphic ones (e.g. ⌐, 9 and ⊓ for 𝕤, ⧸ and ⊏ respectively), as well as for 'diacritic' strokes and dots that served to distinguish between similar-looking cursive signs, but sometimes got 'transferred' to the corresponding hieroglyphs (e.g. ⟨ for ⟨; ⊏ for ⊏). The presence of such signs is in itself not necessarily indicative of insufficient hieroglyphic expertise. Nor does it have to be an indication for the use of cursive master copies in composing hieroglyphic texts (Haring 2010: 33–4).

[41] Compare Näser 2001: 382, on the quality of Eighteenth Dynasty coffins and statuettes from Deir el-Medina, for which see later in this section.

through royal favour or through elite personal relationships (Laboury 2020: 91–2). The artists would have been happy to oblige if their principal tasks left them enough time, and if the 'side jobs' gave them additional income or won them favour with their clients. Among these clients might even be colleagues with complementary expertise, who could be members of the same family or belong to the same community of craftsmen.

Egyptology is fortunate to have abundant evidence in this particular area of knowledge in the form of a community of workmen engaged in constructing and decorating the royal rock tombs in the Valley of the Kings and the Valley of the Queens, near ancient Thebes (modern-day Luxor), during the New Kingdom (1539–1077 BC). The archaeological site of Deir el-Medina, situated in the desert west of the Nile and close to the aforementioned valleys, was the place where these specialized craftsmen were housed with their families. They were expected to spend all of their time working on the king's tomb and were supplied by the government with housing, food rations, clothing, and all equipment needed for their daily work. A supporting staff (*semdet*) including woodcutters, fishermen, water carriers and other workers provided the necessary local products and services. Much of the settlement and its adjoining chapels and workmen's tombs, all situated in the desert, has survived, and the community of necropolis workmen have left a wealth of hieratic texts on papyri and ostraca, in addition to the hieroglyphic inscriptions on the royal and private monuments they produced.[42] Their work on inscribed monuments and objects, the presence of locally based scribes and close contact with government officials resulted in an exceptional level of literacy within this community during the Ramesside Period (1292–1077 BC: Haring 2003; Baines & Eyre 2007: 89–94).[43]

Being specialists in the construction and decoration of monumental rock tombs, the necropolis workmen used their spare time – of which they seem to have had plenty – to create their own monumental tombs, as well as those of their colleagues and superiors, near the settlement (case studies e.g. Keller 2001; Bács 2011). Since several of the workmen were also experts in the production of luxury burial equipment, they made coffins and other funerary furniture for themselves, for each other and for the outside market. The production and exchange of the

---

[42] A large body of literature about this extremely well-documented community has grown in the past decades; see K. Donker van Heel, B. Haring, R. Demarée and J. Toivari-Viitala, *The Deir el-Medina Database*, https://dmd.wepwawet.nl, for an updated systematic bibliography. Brief introductions for non-specialists are Bierbrier (1982) and Andreu-Lanoë and Valbelle (2022). The classical introductions for Egyptologists remain Valbelle (1985) and Černý (2001), now supplemented with the encyclopedic Davies (2018). For the *semdet*, see Gabler (2018). A recent, massive volume of widely different case studies, archaeological and textual (Töpfer, del Vesco & Poole 2022), gives a good impression of the current state of research.

[43] Precise year dates in this text follow Hornung, Krauss and Warburton 2006: 490–5. The reader is reminded that 'precise' is not the same as 'certain'.

latter products within the community and outside is especially well documented and enabled Kathlyn Cooney (2007, 2021) to reconstruct what she dubbed an 'informal workshop'. The private tombs and objects thus produced during the Ramesside Period testify to high artistic standards, and the surviving texts on monuments, papyri and ostraca from this period reflect the excellent literate skills of local scribes and draughtsmen.

The earlier history of the workmen's community at Deir el-Medina (under the Eighteenth Dynasty, 1539–1292 BC) contrasts significantly with their well-documented and highly skilled Ramesside successors.[44] Although the earlier workmen living at the site also engaged in the construction and decoration of royal rock tombs, local literacy and artistic expertise appear to have been limited. There are no locally produced hieratic texts on papyri or ostraca that can securely be dated before circa 1300 BC, and the decorations and hieroglyphic inscriptions on the walls and furniture of local private tombs are of a decidedly lower quality than those of the Ramesside Period. Yet workmen of the Eighteenth Dynasty would have been responsible for the painting of complex religious scenes and inscriptions in the tombs of their kings. It seems likely, therefore, that the specialists who developed the decorative programme of the royal tombs of this period and who controlled its execution were not locally based, and also engaged in (royal) commissions elsewhere.

The rare inscriptions in early monumental tombs of workmen and their superiors, and on objects found with simpler burials near the settlement, testify to very limited skills. Coffins and statuettes from the eastern cemetery of Deir el-Medina have columns of hieroglyphs rendering the usual offering formulas but with many mistakes and omissions (Soliman 2015: 120–1). Coffin Prague Náprstek Museum 627 from tomb DM 1380, for instance, omits some entire words of the offering formula, and parts of others; some signs have been incorrectly selected, positioned or oriented.[45]

Similar mistakes occur on other inscribed coffins and on statuettes from the same cemetery (Näser 2001: 384–8; Soliman 2015: 120–1) and in the hieroglyphic texts of monumental tombs to the west of the settlement, even in that of Kha, the supervisor of royal tomb construction. This official was of high

---

[44] The divide between the early and late phases of the community and their settlement is actually the so-called Amarna Period (1353–1320 BC), during which the settlement may have been (partly) deserted, followed by a reorganization (and possibly repopulation) under King Haremhab. See, for example, Valbelle 1985: 25; compare Haring 2018: 133–5.

[45] Verner 1982: 1/322–9; Soliman 2015: 120–1. The mono-consonantal spelling 𓍢𓄿𓏏𓂋 *ḏ-ḥ-w-t* for 'Thoth' on this coffin instead of the ibis logogram is 𓅝 not necessarily a sign of incompetence here, but may be a convention in funerary inscriptions; compare similar spellings in the names of owners of Middle Kingdom coffins from El-Bersheh (De Buck 1935: xvii).

rank (bearing the title *sš-nswt* 'King's Scribe', reserved for the highest functionaries of the realm) and had exceedingly rich burial equipment and a beautifully painted tomb chapel (Vandier d'Abbadie & Jourdain 1939: pl. II–XVI).[46] The painter of the chapel was highly skilled (Sartori 2022: 657, 659). The individual polychrome hieroglyphs in this chapel, again rendering stereotypical offering formulas, have been made with great care, but orthographic mistakes abound, indicating that whoever *composed* the texts had a very limited understanding of what he was doing (Vandier d'Abbadie & Jourdain 1939: 8–13).

A slightly different case is the tomb chapel of the necropolis workman Amenemhat, possibly dated to the very beginning of the Eighteenth Dynasty (TT 340: Cherpion 1999: 3–55; Laboury 2022: 50–2). Although painted in beautiful colours that are well preserved to this day, the style of the paintings is rather crude, with incorrectly proportioned human and divine figures (Cherpion 1999: pl. 1–23). The scenes on the north and east walls have been left with neither contours nor inscriptions; those on the south and west walls have been finished with contours and with columns of hieroglyphs rendering offering formulas and the names of the persons and deities depicted. Here again, signs and entire words have been omitted and the order of signs and words reversed (see Kruchten 1999 for these and the following observations). Remarkable additional features are (1) the use of mono-consonantal instead of regular orthography (e.g. ⟨ℎ⟩ *j-n-k* or ⟨ℎ⟩ *n-k* for ⟨○⟩ var. ⟨ℎ⟩ *jnk* 'I'/'me');[47] (2) mono-consonantal signs used to abbreviate short words and morphemes (e.g. ⟨ℎ⟩ *r-s* for ⟨ℎ⟩ *rn.sn* 'their names' and ⟨○⟩ *r-f* or reversed ⟨○⟩ *f-r* for ⟨ℎ⟩ *rn.f* 'his name'); (3) multiconsonantal signs with reduced phonetic values (e.g. ⟨ℎ⟩ *ꜥš*ꜣ for *ꜥš* 'call' and ⟨⇒⟩ *tꜣ* for *t*). Features (2) and (3) are reminiscent of acrophony, and in some cases boil down to precisely that (especially *rn > r*), but reduction to strong consonants may be a more correct designation in others (e.g. *ꜥš*ꜣ *> ꜥš*). Together, the features are also reminiscent of orthographies and sign substitutions in enigmatic and Ptolemaic writing (see the previous Section), but the actual signs and spellings used in TT 340 are hardly the same as in those systems.

---

[46] The tomb (TT 8) was discovered intact in 1906; the mummies and burial equipment of Kha and his wife Merit are now in the Museo Egizio, Turin; the chapel has been restored in situ by the French Archaeological Institute (Ifao). See Ferraris 2022 on past and future work on the tomb and its contents.

[47] The spelling ⟨ℎ⟩ was used in the Old Kingdom, which is no surprise given the frequency of mono-consonantal orthography in that period (see Section 2.3), but even at that time, ⟨○⟩ was the preferred writing (Edel 1955–64: 79). The longer writing ⟨ℎ○⟩ with a determinative was used in Middle Egyptian and was especially current in Late Egyptian. The bowl ○ as used in this pronoun is supposed to stand for *jn* (Gardiner 1957: 530).

**Figure 7** Inscription of Sennefer in TT 340. From Cherpion (1999: 44);
reproduced here with kind permission of the publisher.

The maker of these inscriptions, and possibly also the painter of the scenes,
was the tomb owner's son Sennefer. In the caption to a scene depicting himself
making offerings to his parents, Sennefer proudly states: 'I am a son who writes/
paints correctly' (*jnk sꜣ sš mty*), a statement as erroneous as the results of his
work (Figure 7). Rather than a versatile and innovative expert on hieroglyphic
orthography, Sennefer was probably a painter with limited skills, and the
mistakes he made have been plausibly explained by the dearth of correct
examples to copy in the immediate surroundings of TT 340 and the workmen's
settlement in its earliest stages (Kruchten 1999: 54–5; Laboury 2013: 34). The
little he knew about funerary phraseology may have come to his notice solely by
means of short texts on stelae or wooden chests, instead of more elaborate
inscriptions in tombs (Laboury 2020: 89; Sartori 2022: 661). He seems to have
worked with a limited hieroglyphic repertoire, the core of which was mono-
consonantal signs, and invented the writings of some expressions on the spot,
with nothing but their sounds acting as a guideline (Kruchten 1999: 55; Laboury
2022b : 50–2).

Another early Eighteenth Dynasty tomb chapel at Deir el-Medina was never
inscribed, hence its owner remains unknown (TT 354: Cherpion 1999: 57–90).
The style of its decoration is imperfect but not quite to the same degree as
Amenemhat's. It seems that its painter was familiar with iconographic motives

found in elite tombs in the wider Theban necropolis (i.e. not in Deir el-Medina), such as a winged serpent holding a *shen* ring ♀, a symbol of eternity.[48] To this he added emblematic hieroglyphs (⸙ *ankh* and 𝌀 *wadj*), creating a unique iconographic combination, and extended another, ≋ for *mw* 'water', with one more water ripple, creating his own version of the sign: ≣ (Sartori 2022: 668–71). The artist thus shows himself knowledgeable and creative to some extent, but does not demonstrate, and perhaps did not possess, hieroglyphic skills beyond a small group of emblematic signs.

The three early Deir el-Medina tomb chapels discussed here (TT 8, 340 and 354) seem to represent different degrees and combinations of iconographic and literate skills, but in each case, the hieroglyphic knowledge of their makers was limited. The imperfections ranged from mistakes, omissions and highly unusual spellings in texts which remained intelligible nonetheless, to decorations that remained anepigraphic with the exception of a few emblematic hieroglyphs. In all cases, the restricted knowledge of the makers did not stand in the way of their creativity, and it is remarkable that the semi-literate artist of TT 340, when deviating from regular hieroglyphic orthography, used strategies of reduction and substitution not unlike those of the hyper-specialist scribes of enigmatic texts.

## 4.2 Hieroglyphs As Marks: Pseudo-script

The use of hieroglyphs as emblems by Ancient Egyptian craftsmen and their often limited understanding of hieroglyphic texts (Sections 3.1 and 4.1) lead us to another case of extra-textual use of hieroglyphic signs. This is the practice of applying individual marks to objects and stone surfaces. The purposes of such signs include, for instance, the correct positioning of stone blocks, bricks or tiles, marking property, registering the distribution of food rations and tools, signaling work progress, and marking someone's presence in the form of graffiti. Marking systems were used throughout Egyptian history, starting with marks incised or painted on pottery from the mid-third millennium BC onward.[49] The morphology of the earliest pot marks is simple, including individual and multiple strokes, crosses, curves and circles, on rare occasions more complex designs, all traced in the wet clay with fingers or pointed instruments. Prefired pot marks would retain such basic morphology for centuries, and their purposes are difficult to establish. The idea, often considered, that they express the identity of individual potters is

---

[48] For the Eighteenth Dynasty, the motive is otherwise attested only in the tomb of Senneferi (TT 99 in Sheikh Abd el-Qurna, reign of Thutmose III) and on royal statuary and furniture from the reigns of Amenhotep III and Tutankhamen (Sartori 2022: 669–70; Cherpion 1999: 94).

[49] Among the earliest known occurrences are marks on 'rough ware' found at Hierakonpolis (early Naqada II; Hendrickx 2008: 72–4) and on bread moulds found at Adaïma (Naqada III; Bréand 2015).

uncertain, especially given the fact that usually only a small percentage of pottery from a certain period found at the same site is marked (Gallorini 2009: 120–1). The marks need not be about the pottery itself, but may concern the content of the vessels or moulds.[50] Among the repertoire we find signs inspired by hieroglyphs (e.g. ⌶ and ⌣ on late Middle Kingdom pottery from Illahun; Gallorini 2009: 139, 141), but this is very rare. Post-fired pot marks (i.e. marks scratched or painted on pottery after firing) more often show complex forms including several of hieroglyphic inspiration (e.g. ⌷, ⌸, ⌹, ⌺ and ⌻ on Ramesside pottery from Qantir; Ditze 2007: 428–47). The purposes of post-fired marks are also often uncertain. Like prefired marks, they depend on the contexts in which the pottery items (such as vessels and bread moulds) were used originally. In a number of cases, it is clear that post-fired signs express the identity of individuals or institutions who owned the marked vessels; a case in point (property marks of the Deir el-Medina workmen) is described in what follows.

Another marking system with a mixed morphological repertoire is builders' marks. These are signs scratched or painted on stone blocks of temples and pyramids, often in combination with numbers, calendar dates, guiding lines and other notations. The most famous examples are the so-called team marks left on monuments of the Old and Middle Kingdom, and in this case, we can be more certain about their meaning. The individual marks appear to be those of teams of workmen; 'team' representing the smallest division in the organization of workforce in monumental building (Roth 1991: 119–43; Andrássy 2009a; Yamada 2017). Among these team marks we find signs of hieroglyphic inspiration, but also pictorial signs that do not apparently have hieroglyphs as examples,[51] as well as abstract geometric signs (Figure 8). Such a mixed morphology is characteristic of systems of identity marks worldwide.[52] The team marks are a clear case of identity marks, one of the different categories of non-textual marking systems.[53] The identities expressed are those of teams – that is, of collectives. It is often unclear exactly why a specific mark was chosen

---

[50] Marks incised on the inside of Early Dynastic bread moulds from Tell Gabbara were probably meant to leave an impression on the bread baked in the moulds (Rampersad 2020).

[51] It is often difficult to distinguish between hieroglyphic and other pictorial signs, given the iconicity of the hieroglyphic script and its openness to the introduction of new signs (see Section 2.1). See Haring (2018: 31–3, 227–31) for this problem. A clear case of a pictorial but non-hieroglyphic mark is the star or pentagram ⍟; compare the hieroglyphic star ⭑ – also attested as a mark.

[52] Including, for instance, marking systems of European medieval masons (Haring 2018: 63–8) and marks attested on Lydian seals from 6th–4th-century BC Anatolia (Boardman 2010). See the discussions on marking systems in Ancient Egypt and elsewhere collected in Andrássy, Budka and Kammerzell (2009); Haring and Kaper (2009); Evans Pim, Yatsenko and Perrin (2010); Budka, Kammerzell and Rzepka (2015).

[53] For an overview of such notations, see Kammerzell 2009.

**Figure 8** Team marks of the Old and Middle Kingdom. From Andrássy (2009a: 18, figure 9); reproduced here with kind permission of the author and the publisher.

to represent a specific group of people, but some of the hieroglyphic marks may very well be abbreviations of geographical or personal names, and in this way refer to the teams' provenances or supervisors (Andrássy 2009a: 19–22; see also the remarks on P. Reisner II in Section 2.3).

In the early New Kingdom, we see the emergence of similar marking systems used by a construction workforce, but at this time, the marks represent individual workmen.[54] The earliest and best-documented example is that of the Deir el-Medina workmen (see the previous section for these workmen). By the mid-fifteenth century BC at the latest, a system of identity marks was in use in the workmen's settlement and its surroundings, with each mark representing an individual workman (Haring 2018: 158–68; Soliman 2018a). Abundant evidence exists for at least two purposes of the marks at this early stage: marking property (e.g. pottery and textiles; see Figure 9), and composing rudimentary administrative records on ostraca (Figure 10). The latter practice is remarkable in view of the low level of literacy evident in Eighteenth Dynasty Deir el-Medina. As opposed to the thousands of hieratic texts on ostraca or papyri from the Ramesside Period, hieratic texts that can be ascribed with certainty to the community of workmen living at the site prior to that period seem to be non-existent (Haring 2006), and inscriptions on local tomb walls and funerary artifacts betray a very limited knowledge of hieroglyphic orthography (see Section 4.1).

Given this apparently poor state of local literacy, one might be led to think that the use of marks on ostraca, often in clusters and accompanied by additional data in the form of dots or strokes so as to form a sort of pseudo-script, was a mere replacement for actual writing. This is probably true in the sense that, as

---

[54] An earlier existence of marks referring to individual members of a construction workforce is possible but highly uncertain; see Andrássy 2009a: 22–5.

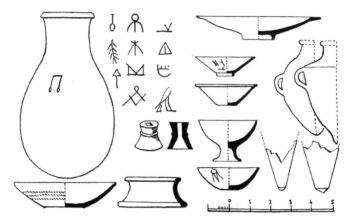

**Figure 9** Marked pottery from Deir el-Medina, Eighteenth Dynasty. From Bruyère (1953: pl. XXII); reproduced here with kind permission of the publisher.

**Figure 10** Ostracon Cairo CG 24105, Eighteenth Dynasty. From Daressy (1902: pl. XVIII).

opposed to writing, the marking system was known to all workmen (since every single member of the workforce had his mark) and could thus potentially be used by every one of them for any purpose. Indeed, the marks on many ostraca are crude in form and have been made with thick brushes (such as were used for the painting of tomb walls), indicating that they were actually made by the workmen themselves or by semi-literate supervisors (e.g. Soliman 2018a: figures 2–5, 7 – bottom row, 9–10). Only on a few ostraca do we see neat hieroglyphic graphs among the marks (e.g. Soliman 2018a: figures 1, 6, 7 – top row, 8), presumably made by draughtsmen using finer brushes.

The assumption, plausible in itself, that the administrative 'texts' with marks on ostraca compensated for the absence of actual writing skills, is to be modified by the evidence from the Ramesside Period. Thousands of locally produced hieratic texts on papyri and (mainly) ostraca testify to the exceptional spread of literacy in the workmen's community in this later phase of the New Kingdom. But the production of ostraca bearing workmen's marks did not stop or diminish in that period; on the contrary, the growing production of hieratic ostraca during the Nineteenth and early Twentieth Dynasties was paralleled by a growing number of ostraca inscribed with marks and by the appearance of a more intricate pseudo-script – that is, a complex notation combining marks with other sorts of signs (Figure 11). A similar development can be seen in graffiti left by the workmen and their superiors throughout the Theban necropolis. The very habit of making graffiti, textual or in the form of identity marks, seems to have started in the workmen's community in the Ramesside Period, and the use of marks for identity purposes kept pace with the hieratic and hieroglyphic graffiti. Workmen could basically use any of these systems for noting their presence in the Theban mountains; some graffiti are even combinations of marks and writing (Fronczak & Rzepka 2009; Rzepka 2015). The use of marks on ostraca and as graffiti seems to have been stimulated, rather than marginalized, by the spread of writing, and

**Figure 11** Ostracon Glasgow D.1925.80, obverse. From McDowell (1993: pl. XX); reproduced here with kind permission of the author and the publisher. The marks ⟨ and ⟩ (in black) are visible in the right column, fifth and fourth lines from the bottom. The marks ⟨ and ⟨ (in outline, indicating red paint in the original) are in the left column, third and fifth lines from the top.

many of the ostraca may have been produced by a small group of semi-literate 'scribes' supporting the regular administrators who compiled hieratic accounts of the progress of work at the king's tomb and of the supplies necessary for that work and for the upkeep of the workmen and their families (see Soliman 2018b for the possible identification of two such 'scribes').

One other feature of the Deir el-Medina marks suggests that their creation and use were stimulated by the growth of writing skills among the workmen. This is reflected by the increasing proportion, in the sign repertoire, of marks inspired by hieroglyphs. Whereas some 50 to 60 per cent of the Eighteenth Dynasty marks appear to have had a hieroglyphic origin, by the mid-Twentieth Dynasty, that percentage had risen to approximately 85 (Haring 2018: 234), as well as being supplemented by some marks with hieratic inspiration (e.g. ⪦ and 𝕪). The role of hieratic would remain marginal in the graphic repertoire of the marks themselves. The distinctive forms and visual appeal of the hieroglyphic script made it the dominant inspiration for the marks. This is also clear from ostraca where marks are presented in vertical columns, sometimes even with framing lines. This was the usual format of monumental hieroglyphic inscriptions in temples and tombs, but it had been abandoned in hieratic writing after the Middle Kingdom.

But what determined the choice of specific hieroglyphs as prototypes of marks? In the quasi-absence of written information about the Eighteenth Dynasty gangs of workmen and their individual members, it is difficult to say what connected a specific mark to its user. The few marks of this period that can be connected to men we know by name include that of the overseer Kha (see Section 4.1), which appears to be non-hieroglyphic: ⅄. It is attested on items of Kha's burial equipment, as well as on pottery from the settlement and on ostraca (Figure 9).[55]

With the Ramesside marks we are on firmer ground due to the massive presence of written documentation from that period, which enables us to follow the workmen and their families during multiple generations. In fact, many marks turn out to be family marks. By way of example, we may look at ⅄, a mark derived from the hieroglyph representing a hoe, with phonetic value *mr*. At some point in the late Nineteenth or early Twentieth Dynasty, this mark was held by a workman called Meryre (*Mry-Rˁ*). The mark would therefore seem to be a reference to the workman's name. It is indeed possible that the mark was first used by this workman, or by an ancestor of his with the same name. When Meryre's son Neferhotep took up his position as a necropolis workman, the latter adopted a different mark: ⊓, inspired by the hieroglyph ▭ depicting the sky. There is no obvious relation, phonetic or

---

[55] Soliman 2015: 110–11. Possible but uncertain connections, suggested by their occurrences in the western cemetery of Deir el-Medina, are those of a man called Hekanakht with the mark 𓅯 (apparently a non-hieroglyphic sign), and of a Nekhunefer with 𓏞 (possibly representing a mirror, but not necessarily a hieroglyph). Compare Soliman 2015: 124 and 126.

semantic, between the mark (or hieroglyph) and the name Neferhotep. Just like ⑂, the mark may have had a longer history in the family of Neferhotep and his father – we do not know what marks were used by earlier generations of this family. Neferhotep's two sons, also called Meryre and Neferhotep, had the marks ⊓ and ⑂ respectively. When a son of the latter Neferhotep, who was called Meryre, became a workman, he took over his father's mark ⑂ .[56] Thus we see that only the earliest and the last mentioned Meryre held a mark related to their name. The mark skipped one generation after the earliest Meryre and was then held by a person called Neferhotep. The marks are therefore not name signs, but personal marks transmitted (mainly) within families. The reason that Neferhotep son of Meryre did not inherit his father's mark was probably that he and his father were active as workmen together and the latter still held his personal mark ⑂. Only when Meryre stopped working or passed away did his mark become available, and it was taken by his grandson Neferhotep. The latter passed it on directly to his son Meryre. It is probably Neferhotep or his son Meryre who is represented by the mark on an ostracon from the reign of Ramesses IV or V (Figure 11).

Such intricacies have become clear through research carried out at Leiden University, mainly by comparing hundreds of ostraca bearing marks with the prosopographical data obtained from hieratic and hieroglyphic texts from Deir el-Medina.[57] Marks were transmitted within families, often skipping a generation and then reappearing when a grandfather passed on his mark to a grandson or to a different member of the family. Occasionally, a mark could even go to a workman of a different family if he took the place of an unrelated colleague. Marks were therefore not always tied to the names of their holders, but it was their relationship with personal names that led to the first identifications of Deir el-Medina marks and to the understanding of their transmission (Haring 2000). An additional help was the fact that in hieratic texts from Deir el-Medina, the names of workmen often appear in fixed sequences, especially in the so-called duty roster, a rota in which every single day a specific workman was required to attend to the formal reception of supplies and other matters (Haring 2015b). The same rota is reflected on ostraca combining workmen's marks with administrative data. By comparing the two types of sources, with the assumption that some of the marks were related to the names of the workmen, matches could be found between the sequences of marks and those of names in the hieratic texts.

---

[56] See Haring 2018: 218–19 for these persons and their marks. In Deir el-Medina prosopography, they are numbered Meryre (v), Neferhotep (xi), Meryre (vi), Neferhotep (xii) and Meryre (vii) respectively; see Davies 1999: 229–34 and chart 20.

[57] Including a four-year research project (2011–15) funded by the Netherlands Organisation for Scientific Research (NWO). The research team consisted of Kyra van der Moezel, Daniel Soliman and the author. See Haring 2018: ix–xi.

The first such match was made with an ostracon of the early Twentieth Dynasty and involved the marks 𓄟 (*ms*) of a workman called Mose, 𓅃 (a falcon, 'Horus') of a man called Hor, and † (*wsr*) of someone called Userhat. Two other marks provided indirect confirmation: 𓏏 of Neferhotep and ⊔ of Penanuqet. The former was Neferhotep son of Meryre, whom we have already discussed. Penanuqet had the mark ⊔ and a father, Kasa, whose name starts with ⊔ (*k3*). It seemed plausible therefore that Neferhotep and Penanuqet inherited their fathers' marks, and this was borne out by subsequent research (Haring 2018: 5–10, 185–6). In all five cases, the marks were graphic reductions of the written names of the holders or of their fathers – or, theoretically, of earlier ancestors. The hieroglyphs that were the inspiration for the marks were the first signs used in the hieroglyphic and hieratic writing of the corresponding names.

However, the majority of marks in the duty roster, and hence the majority of marks used within the community of workmen, cannot be connected with the names of the holders or of their ancestors. For some of the hieroglyphic marks this may be due to our lack of knowledge about the names of remote ancestors of some of the workmen. But in the case of marks that are non-hieroglyphic, there may be no intrinsic connection at all. The repertoire of marks also includes pictorial signs that are probably not hieroglyphs, such as depictions of a jar, a headrest or a jackal. One or more necropolis workmen of the Twentieth Dynasty used the jar as their personal mark. The graphic variety of individual examples of this mark is great, and includes jars with and without handles, and with or without liquid issuing from the jar (e.g. ⟡, 𓎯, 𓏊). Such specific features were significant in the hieroglyphic script, but apparently, they were less important in the marking system. It might well be, therefore, that the mark was 'jar' as a concrete notion, rather than a reference to a specific hieroglyph. This is all the more understandable given the massive presence of ceramic vessels in and around the workmen's settlement. The same point may be made with respect to the headrest 𓊪, a common piece of furniture in the workmen's households and in their burial equipment, but extremely rare as a hieroglyph.[58] The proper names of necropolis workmen called 'The Jar' or 'The Headrest' are unknown to us; nor do we find such designations among their nicknames.[59] One clear case of reference to a nickname is the jackal 𓃥, which we know to have been held by a workman called Amennakht nicknamed 'The Jackal'. Amennakht was a son of Hay, a deputy to

---

[58] See Haring 2009: 127–32; 2018: 31–3, 228–9, for these and other concrete, non-hieroglyphic marks. The distinction between 'concrete' referents and hieroglyphic ones is also made in discussions of the Proto-Sinaitic script; see Goldwasser 2006: 135–51, and Section 5.3.

[59] Members of the community's supporting workforce (of woodcutters etc., see Section 4.1) included at least one called *P3-ds* 'The (Beer) Jar'; his name was written 𓎯 or semi-phonetic 𓊪𓎯 *P(3)-ds* in pseudo-written texts on ostraca, for which see later in this section.

one of the chief workmen. Hay's mark was a pomegranate ⸚, a mark that had been in his family for generations, but when his son Amennakht became a necropolis workman, Hay was still active. The pomegranate mark was therefore not available. Amennakht 'The Jackal' seems to have created his own mark, referring to his nickname. When he was promoted to the position of deputy, possibly upon the death of his father, he adopted the pomegranate that had been his family's mark for a long time, which had now also become a reference for his father's and his own high status. The jackal mark, on the contrary, disappeared after its short period of use by the 'mere' workman Amennakht (Haring 2018: 209–11).

In cases where the hieroglyphic origin of many Deir el-Medina marks is clear to us, it was not always so to the minds of the ancient users. The marks give us a very precious clue to the impact hieroglyphs had on an Ancient Egyptian community, even on an exceptionally literate one. It is clear that within the community of necropolis workmen, the extent and sorts of literacy varied greatly. One extreme of the spectrum was professional scribes and draughts-men, who were perfectly capable of composing and realizing hieratic and hieroglyphic texts. The other extreme was barely literate workmen, who were nonetheless in frequent contact with hieroglyphs, seeing them on a daily basis. It would, in fact, have been almost impossible to live on the Theban west bank of the Nile with its numerous inscribed tombs and temples, to be housed in or near a settlement where hieroglyphic inscriptions and hieratic ostraca were omni-present, and yet to be totally illiterate. But the ability to make sense of texts must have varied considerably. As we have seen in Section 4.1, even the artists involved in the decoration and inscription of the local tombs of Deir el-Medina included craftsmen with limited knowledge who were not capable of writing correct hieroglyphic texts, but who could do partially correct funerary formulae, or at least some important hieroglyphic emblems.

It is instructive to observe, then, that the 'scribes' who created the ostraca featuring workmen's marks in combination with other sorts of signs partly derived from writing, often failed to recognize the hieroglyphic and hieratic prototypes of the signs they wrote. The falcon mark held by the workman Hor is a case in point. The shape of the mark as it appears in the pseudo-written duty rosters is rarely reminiscent of a falcon, although clearly representing a bird (Figure 11). Here, as with the non-hieroglyphic jar (see the previous paragraph), the precise form of the sign was apparently not of vital importance, notwith-standing the hieroglyphic reference to the holder's name in the case of the 'falcon'. In the few cases where a falcon may actually be recognized, the sign takes on a hieratic rather than hieroglyphic shape. This ties in well with the hieratic inspiration for other signs used on the pseudo-script ostraca, consisting chiefly of numbers.

Hieratic inspiration seems to be absent in the use of marks on Eighteenth Dynasty ostraca, which is not surprising given the very low presence of local literacy at Deir el-Medina in that period. Equally unsurprising is that on those ostraca too the hieroglyphic origin of some marks was not recognized. Among clusters of Eighteenth Dynasty marks we find  (with variants , ; the precise number of strokes underneath was apparently of no importance). Only after comparison of clusters of marks and their sequence on many different ostraca did it become clear that the sign was inspired by the necklace , hieroglyph for 'gold'(*nbw*) (Haring 2018: 33, 229–30). If this identification had not been made, the rather abstract graph  might have been reckoned among the non-pictorial, geometric marks. The sign is illustrative of a larger group of marks that are difficult to accommodate in the tripartite morphology (writing – concrete – geometric) of the workmen's marks, and of the 'fuzzy borders' between the three morphological categories.

One last example may be given to illustrate the graphic diversity of marks that was the result of not recognizing their hieroglyphic origin. Several ostraca from the late Twentieth Dynasty show very similar sequences of marks. One side of ostracon Brooklyn Museum 16.118 is graphically divided in a number of cells so as to form a table, each cell containing a depiction of an activity or a commodity, with marks to indicate the workmen responsible, whose names we do not know. The workman represented by  and the figure of a man holding a mat was apparently supposed to produce or supply a mat,  was to paint or brush (as implied by the depiction of a brush or broom), and  was to produce or supply furniture (a bed and a headrest). The first two marks clearly derive from hieroglyphs; the third as well if it is a doubling of  *ankh*. Combinations of these marks with others are found on other ostraca from the same period – for example,  (Ifao ONL 6480);  (Ifao OL 170); [...]  (Ashmolean Museum HO 1098).[60] There appears to be a fixed order in these sequences of marks, but the sign following  is different on all ostraca: . Yet these graphs are somehow similar and seem to be graphic variants. It may well be that one of them was the mark as originally conceived, and inspired by either  *ankh* (*ʿnḫ*) or  *nefer* (*nfr*). Both signs were exceedingly popular as marks throughout pharaonic history, and in the crude style that usually characterises their non-hieroglyphic use, they could easily be confused. As an isolated mark, one would be practically identical with the other when turned upside down (), as would happen often with property marks on movable objects. This is how confusion may have come about. Although it

[60] All of these ostraca await publication. A catalogue of Ifao ostraca is being prepared by Kyra van der Moezel, Daniel Soliman and the author, to be published by the Institut français d'archéologie orientale (Ifao) in Cairo.

remains difficult to explain why some specimens show multiple ⸗ or ⸗, the sign sequences on the ostraca mentioned do seem to indicate that they were mere graphic variants (allographs) of one and the same mark. Unfortunately, we do not know which workman was its holder.

Since the principal topic of this Element is the impact of hieroglyphs on their makers and readers, little has been said in the previous paragraphs about the other sorts of signs used on ostraca featuring the necropolis workmen's identity marks. The combinations of signs used in the particular pseudo-script of Ramesside ostraca include numerical notations inspired by hieratic numbers and pictograms for items delivered: firewood, fish, dates and loaves of bread. A typical entry consists of a calendar date starting with the pseudo-hieroglyphic ⎮ for *s(w)* 'day' followed by a number in hieratic, the mark of a workman on day duty and pictograms with numbers for the commodities supplied. For instance, the full entry on ostracon Glasgow D.1925.80, obverse, fourth line from the bottom, reads: 'Day 12. Meryre (or: Neferhotep), *pesen*-loaves 8, *bit*-loaves 4, (one unit of) dates (for) the left side' (Figure 11). Some entries mention the delivering persons, who were members of the community's supporting work-force (*semdet*). The first, second and fifth lines of the right column on the same ostracon end with: '300 (units of firewood), *ms*.' The last sign in all three cases is a crude form of 𓀔 standing for *ms*. This would seem to be the mark of the necropolis workman Mose mentioned earlier in this section, who was actually active at the time this ostracon was produced. In fact, that workman is repre-sented by his mark in the third line of the left column. The *ms* indicated three times in the right column was not the necropolis workman, but a woodcutter called 'Ptahmose', who supplied the firewood referred to by the number '300'. Careful analysis of the numerous pseudo-script ostraca like Glasgow D.1925.80 makes clear that the entries of such ostraca had their own fixed 'syntax', in which not only the shape but also the position of signs was decisive for their meaning. Thus, the mark 𓀔 stands for the necropolis workman Mose only at the beginning of an entry (i.e. following immediately after the calendar date), whereas at the end of entries (following the amounts of firewood delivered), 𓀔 indicates a woodcutter called 'Ptahmose'. The pseudo-script can therefore be considered a notation of double articulation, like writing (see Section 2.1), although it was not writing in the strict sense of the word. With the exception of ⎮ for *s(w)* 'day', none of the signs or sign combinations is language-specific. Instead, reference is made directly to persons (through marks), commodities (pictograms) and numbers.

'Pseudo-script' is a term applied in scholarly literature to different sorts of notations which have one thing in common: they resemble writing without sharing all the characteristics of writing (Kammerzell 2009: 298–301).

The particular type of pseudo-script discussed in this section has important features in common with hieroglyphic and hieratic writing. It puts signs resembling hieroglyphic and hieratic characters and numbers in horizontal sequences, and it conveys messages by specific combinations of such signs in a set order. Some of its signs even refer to specific words or names: the sign for *sw* 'day', and a limited number of signs reflecting personal names, including identity marks. The sign used for the woodcutter Ptahmose is not an identity mark – that is, the woodcutter himself would not have used 𓀲 as such. Instead, it was an abbreviation used by the composers of the pseudo-script ostraca in addition to abbreviations for other delivering members of the *semdet* workforce. As said earlier, these composers were probably limited in number and supported the scribes of hieratic documents with what may have been preliminary records, using a notation that was accessible to semi-literate 'scribes' in the workplace. Since the records they produced are about deliveries typically made by the *semdet*, the composers may have been known in the Deir el-Medina community as '*semdet* scribes', a title rarely attested in the hieratic texts and possibly referring to a category of administrators coordinating the *semdet* supplies (Davies 1999: 140–2; Gabler 2018: 412–35; Soliman 2018b).

In this section on marks and pseudo-script, the focus has been on Deir el-Medina because the amount and documentation of relevant material, and the archaeological and historical context provided by the site, present the best basis for a case study. Although the extent of its use in this particular setting was exceptional, the marking system itself was not. Similar signs occur as property marks and builders' marks throughout pharaonic history,[61] as may have become clear from the discussion of pot marks and builders' marks at the beginning of this section. Even the use of marks as components of pseudo-written codes was not restricted to Deir el-Medina nor to the New Kingdom. Very recently, examples from later periods have come to the attention of Egyptologists. A pottery vase from the seventh or sixth century BC is inscribed with entries that each consist of a calendar date followed by several lines of pseudo(?)-hieratic text together with geometric and pictorial signs, the latter partly hieroglyphic (Cairo JE 56283; Vittmann 2022). Some of the signs might be marks of a nature similar to the Deir el-Medina ones, but the entire text resists decipherment with exception of the dates. Among the thousands of Demotic ostraca from the late

---

[61] For example, temple blocks (*talatat*) in El-Amarna and Hermopolis inscribed with hieroglyphic and geometric marks probably represent individual masons (Haring 2018: 52–3). Marks on architectural elements may also have served for their correct positioning, such as the hiero-glyphic marks on the ram sphinxes in front of the Karnak temples of Amun-Re and Khonsu, which are probably connected with their (re-)positioning by the priest-king Pinodjem I (Cabrol 1995: 21–3).

Ptolemaic and early Roman Period found in and near the Athribis temple precinct are several inscribed with Demotic calendar dates and numbers in combination with signs of hieroglyphic appearance that might also be identity marks.[62]

There are other types of pseudo-script, including one referred to as 'asemic' writing. 'Asemic' is not to be taken here in the literal sense of 'meaningless', but rather in the sense that a piece of writing is not supposed to convey any particular message other than the apparent fact that it is writing: 'A composition in pseudo script may even be void of actual meaning and deliberately function as a mere sequence of *indexical signs* which transport nothing but the message that the producer makes use of "writing"' (Kammerzell 2009: 299, referring to the entire compositions as 'textograms'). Examples from Ancient Egypt include private funerary 'inscriptions' on coffins of the Third Intermediate Period and mummy shrouds of the Roman Period, which look like hieroglyphic texts, but on closer inspection appear to be incoherent groupings of (pseudo-)hieroglyphic signs (Figure 12).[63] What is true for the limited understanding of hieroglyphs discussed in Section 4.1 is certainly true for these pseudo-hieroglyphic texts: 'Because of the seemingly pictographic character of the hieroglyphic script it appeals much more to the eye of the beholder, especially if that person is *not* able to read the text as a *text* in a non-pictographic way' (Von Lieven 2009: 107).

There is bound to be more material awaiting research on this topic. Scholars tend to focus on material they can make sense of, and until a few decades ago, even the Deir el-Medina marking system was not among such material. Its resistance to regular hieroglyphic interpretation caused Egyptologists to refer to the marks as 'funny signs' (e.g. Parkinson 1999: 93 and 96) and led to the marginalization of the rich material available, which was left undocumented in dusty cupboards and basements, whereas numerous catalogues were produced of hieroglyphic and hieratic inscriptions from the same site. Unpublished material excavated at Deir el-Medina and other sites includes types of visual expression we still fail to understand, which will achieve their proper place in scholarly literature only when researchers find sufficient clues to their meaning and appropriate labels for their categorization.

---

[62] I am grateful to Sandra Lippert for drawing my attention to these ostraca, and for showing me images of some of them. They are as yet unpublished, as are the majority of the Athribis ostraca; see Boud'hors et al. 2021: 84–112.

[63] Von Lieven 2009: 104–5; among the examples given there are coffins 27 and 54 + 64 from the tomb of Iurudef at Saqqara (Raven 1991: 23, pl. 37), and shroud Berlin inv. 8/65 (Bresciani 1996: 50–1). Von Lieven also refers to funerary monuments 'inscribed' with columns or lines that were left empty or merely filled with hatching (2009: 108–9).

**Figure 12** Pseudo-hieroglyphic text on coffin 54 + 64 from the tomb of Iurudef at Saqqara. From Raven (1991: pl. 37); reproduced here with kind permission of the author and the publisher.

## 5 Hieroglyphs Abroad: Non-Egyptian Notations and Scripts Inspired by Hieroglyphs

Most readers will be familiar to some extent with the great impact Egyptian material culture, iconography and hieroglyphic writing has had on later cultural traditions, both in Europe and in the Middle East. It will come as no surprise, then, that such impact was equally great, if not greater, on Egypt's immediate neighbours (Nubia and the Levant) during pharaonic times. Its manifestation was not continuously so overt nor displayed the same characteristics in all adjoining regions, but correlated with the intensity and nature of contacts between the societies involved. Thus, the use of pharaonic iconography and writing in Levantine material culture became particularly prominent in the Middle Bronze Age (*c.*2000–1600 BC, roughly contemporary with the

Egyptian Middle Kingdom), while Egyptian-style objects and inscriptions produced by Nubians are mainly known from the eighth century BC onward. In both cases, foreign immigration and rulership *in* Egypt were important stimuli for the adoption of Egyptian culture in the regions of origin.

In the Middle Bronze Age, immigration from the Levant into northern Egypt became significant and led to changes in domestic, religious and urban architecture, as well as burial customs, in settlements of the eastern Nile Delta. The new features (such as distinctive types of pottery, walled settlements and burials of warriors with equids and weapons) link the region with Middle Bronze Age cultures in the Levant. Thus they testify to a certain cultural continuum extending from the Levant into Egyptian state-defined territory until the end of the Middle Kingdom, when the political configuration changed. A dynasty of Levantine descent arose in Avaris (present-day Tell el-Daba), in the centre of the eastern Nile Delta, and conquered the north of Egypt as far as Kis (El-Kusiya). South of this region the Theban Sixteenth and Seventeenth Dynasties held power – though at some point were possibly a vassal state of the northern rulers. These foreign rulers adopted the Egyptian expressions (ornaments, titles and epithets) of pharaonic kingship, but retained their Semitic names and insisted on calling themselves 'Rulers of Foreign Countries' in Egyptian: ⬚ *ḥqꜣ ḫꜣswt*, a designation transcribed as 'Hyksos' in later classical sources. Inscribed objects featuring the names and titles of Hyksos kings, especially scarab amulets (see the following section), became distributed throughout a wide area, as far as Nubia in the south and to Syria and Crete in the north. The Hyksos were defeated by the Theban king Ahmose (1539–1515 BC), who reunited Egypt and ended what Egyptologists call the Second Intermediate Period. He and his successors conducted frequent military campaigns in the Levant during the following Eighteenth Dynasty, thus inaugurating a new phase in Egypto-Levantine relations. The impact of Egyptian hieroglyphs in the Levant in the period before the rise of the Eighteenth Dynasty will be discussed in Sections 5.1–3.

Nubia, on the other side of Egypt, had been colonized by the pharaohs of the Twelfth Dynasty as far as the Second Cataract (near present Wadi Halfa), south of which the powerful kingdom of Kush asserted itself. During the Second Intermediate Period, Kush dominated northern Nubia, threatened the Theban kingdom and was in contact with the Hyksos kings. By the beginning of the Eighteenth Dynasty, the Theban kings had defeated Kush, and a century later, Egyptian territory stretched further south, with Egyptian towns and temples built along the banks of the Nubian Nile. Napata became the southernmost Egyptian stronghold with monumental temples, located approximately 100 kilometres from the Fourth Cataract. Until the End of the New Kingdom (1077 BC), Nubia would remain a colony administered by an Egyptian governor, the 'King's Son of Kush'. Throughout the periods of Kushite and Egyptian domination, the local Nubian population does not seem to have embraced Egyptian material and visual culture. Their elite did not present themselves in Egyptian-style monuments and depictions, nor by writing hieroglyphic texts. In the centuries following the end of the New Kingdom, however, a Nubian kingship developed that built on the Egyptian model, with Napata as its political centre and the cult of Amun at the core of its religious ideology. From the far south, King Piye and his successors conquered Egypt in the late eighth century BC, and ruled their Nubian-Egyptian empire as thoroughly Egyptianized pharaohs. After the Assyrians had driven their dynasty (the Twenty-Fifth) from Egypt, their Egyptian-style kingship continued in the far south of Nubia and developed into the Meroitic kingdom which lasted into the Roman Period.

From the start of the Twenty-Fifth Dynasty, the Nubian pharaohs used the Egyptian language and hieroglyphic script for their inscriptions, with their personal names functioning as the single expression of their own language, just as the Hyksos kings had done. Only in the third century BC did Nubian kings ruling from Meroe, further to the south, adapt Egyptian scripts for writing their own language (called 'Meroitic'). The present state of investigation suggests that this process started with a cursive Meroitic script inspired by Egyptian Demotic, the latter script supposedly having been used in Meroe for centuries (Rilly 2022: 4–5).[64] The next step was the development of a monumental hieroglyphic script, the signs of which were all borrowed from Egyptian hiero-glyphic (Figure 13). For many of the borrowed signs, the Egyptian phonetic values were relevant as well – for example, 𓊡 (Egyptian biconsonantal: *bꜣ*, Meroitic *b*), 𓂝𓏤 (*l*) and 𓄿 (*m*).[65] But Meroitic hieroglyphs are not mono-consonantal nor biconsonantal signs. The set of twenty-three hieroglyphs (corresponding to as many cursive signs) is an alphasyllabary, a syllabic script based on an alphabetic set of sounds. More specifically, it is an *abugida*, which means that most signs represent syllables of the type consonant + vowel /a/, unless they are followed by signs indicating other specific vowels (Daniels 2018: 67; Rilly 2022: 8). Thus these three signs represent *ba*, *la* and *ma*, but may be accompanied by signs representing vowels, such as 𓏲 *i* or 𓏭 *e*, thus changing the syllables to *bi/be* and so forth.[66] The Meroitic scripts are thus fundamentally different from the Egyptian

---

[64] Several, but not all, of the Meroitic cursive signs seem to be graphically inspired by Demotic signs or groups for single consonants, with corresponding phonetic references (cf. Rilly 2022: 2, figure 1 with Johnson 1991: 2–4).

[65] In some cases, the reason for the connection between sign and sound remains elusive – for example, 𓂧 for *d* and 𓎡 for *k* (Rilly 2022: 6). The signs are rendered here in Egyptian hieroglyphic font (JSesh); for more precise Meroitic forms, see Rilly (2022: 2) and Rilly and De Voogt (2012: 58–9).

[66] See Rilly (2022: 2) for the sign repertoire and Rilly and De Voogt (2012: 35–61) for an in-depth analysis.

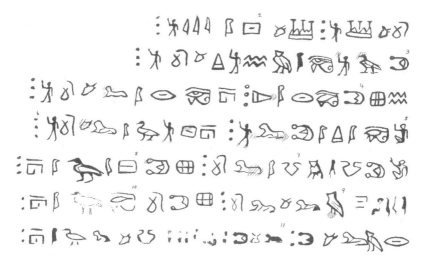

**Figure 13** Hieroglyphic inscription on offering table Berlin 2255 from Meroe pyramid A 28. After Griffith (1911: pl. XXXII, no. 60).

ones from which they took their inspiration. The repertoire of signs had been reduced to a limited set of phonograms that is used in a way that is totally different from Egyptian hieroglyphs and Demotic. In addition, Meroitic signs are not oriented towards the beginning of the line like Egyptian hieroglyphs, but look towards the end, and a special sign (three dots arranged vertically for hieroglyphic, two for cursive Meroitic) is used as word divider. Claude Rilly considers the Meroitic hieroglyphic script an invention 'by one or several scribes', the cursive script having naturally developed from Demotic (Rilly 2022: 6).

## 5.1 Emblematic Signs and Hieroglyphic Pseudo-Script in the Levant

From Early Dynastic times onward, trade and diplomatic relations between Egypt and the Levant brought Egyptian material culture, including objects inscribed with hieroglyphic texts, to important Levantine urban centres such as Byblos and Ebla. In the Middle Bronze Age, hieroglyphs and elements of Egyptian iconography appear on locally produced objects, notably on amulets and seals. In the northern Levant ('Syria'), where Mesopotamian culture dominated, hieroglyphs and other Egyptian symbols were sometimes included in the decoration of otherwise Mesopotamian style cylinder seals.[67] In the southern Levant

---

[67] See Teissier 1996 for examples. 'Syria' and 'Palestine' are conventional names used in Egyptology as references to the Levant, also in combination ('Syria-Palestine'), and as such have no modern political implications.

('Palestine'), we find seals and amulets more overtly inspired by Egyptian models, especially scarabs, amulets in the shape of the dung beetle, which was an important Egyptian symbol of creation. Inscriptions or iconographic motifs were incised into the flat bases of scarabs so they could also be used as stamp seals. Scarabs appeared as amulets in Egypt in the First Intermediate Period (*c.*2100–1980 BC), and were increasingly preferred as stamp seals in the centuries that followed. Stamp seals of other types are already attested in the Old Kingdom, in addition to the cylinder seals that had been shared with Mesopotamia since predynastic times. Both cylinder seals and stamp seals could display hieroglyphic inscriptions (such as the names of royalty or administrators), but also other pictorial signs or abstract motifs. Harco Willems argues that the non-hieroglyphic repertoire of Egyptian seals follows an unbroken tradition from the late predynastic period, and is to be associated with a 'cultural substratum' (Willems 2018: 197–9). Some seal impressions show meaningless groupings of hieroglyphs, a sort of pseudo-script (Willems 2018: figures 2–3, 6–7; see Section 4.2 for the notion of pseudo-script). One may surmise, then, that the makers of seals included semi-literates who were familiar with (some) hieroglyphic signs but unable to compose correct texts.

Egyptian scarabs were imported from Egypt in the Levant, but also produced locally – and the difference is not always obvious. The earliest 'Palestine' scarabs appear about 1700 BC (in the transition from Middle Bronze IIA to IIB; Keel 2004). The decoration of their bases typically includes Egyptian iconography and hieroglyphs, but not always in the specific combinations we know from formal Egyptian art and inscriptions. Although as objects they were inspired by Egyptian examples, the Levantine scarabs followed their own conventions, in which signs borrowed from a range of locations became part of new compositions. The borrowed elements came mainly from Egypt, but also from other regions: some Palestine scarabs, for instance, show motifs otherwise known only in Anatolia (Keel 2004: 79).

Hieroglyphs were particularly favoured as components of visual compositions on Levantine scarabs. The signs selected include, on the one hand, emblematic signs that were also used as such in Egyptian iconography, such as ☥ *ankh*, 𓊽 *djed* and 𓄤 *nefer*, and specific royal or divine emblems such as crowns (e.g. 𓋔) and cobras (𓆗). It may be asked if Levantine observers recognized these as signs of writing, but the same question could also be asked concerning Egyptian signs. When working with such signs, even Egyptian specialists producing formal iconography and inscriptions minimized the difference between writing and image (see Figure 5 in Section 3.1). The initiated observer would know what to read as text and which signs to take in as non-textual icons or symbols (see Section 3.1). To the less knowledgeable

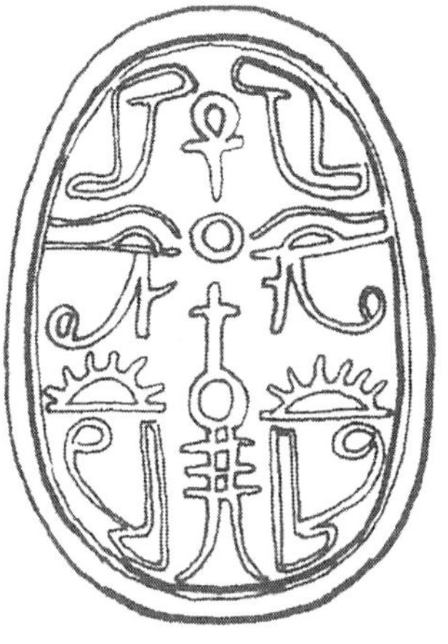

**Figure 14** Levantine scarab with Egyptian iconography. From Keel (2004: 74, no. 2); reproduced here with kind permission of the author and the publisher.

Egyptian, making that distinction would be more difficult, and the same is true for the Levantine producers of Egyptian-inspired imagery. Some combinations of signs closely follow Egyptian examples (Keel 2004: 74; Ben-Tor 2009: 94; see Figure 14). Others defy interpretation along strict Egyptian (or Egyptological) lines. A very clear example is 𓉡, a common Egyptian writing of the name of the goddess Hathor. Signs inspired by this particular hieroglyph were popular on Levantine scarabs, yet it is doubtful if their producers and users saw in it the same reference as denoted by the Egyptian prototype, the more so since the sign could be deconstructed so as to represent a falcon and what appears to be a loose element in the shape of an angle, instead of a falcon within an enclosure (Figure 15). The falcon itself may therefore have become the actual sign (perhaps even as a reference to Horus or another specific deity), instead of the original Egyptian composite (Goldwasser 2006: 121–30). The broader combinations of signs in which it features too do not precisely follow Egyptian configurations.

On the other hand, we find repeated use of sign groups resembling hieroglyphic ones, even including signs of very low iconicity, but without apparent reference to linguistic expressions. The best known of these groupings among specialists, and very popular in the Levantine Middle Bronze Age, are the 'anra' groups, so called because they look like combinations of the Egyptian hieroglyphs 𓂝 (ʿ), 𓈖 (*n*), and 𓂋 (*r*) (Figure 16; full treatment in Richards 2001). Since the precise sequences of these signs can vary, yet they seem to mimic groups of hieroglyphs, they may be regarded as pseudo-script. Although we

**Figure 15** Levantine scarab with reinterpretations of Egyptian hieroglyphs. From Keel (2004: 88, no. 60); reproduced here with kind permission of the author and the publisher.

**Figure 16** 'Anra' scarab. From Ben-Tor (2007: pl. 82, no. 2); reproduced here with kind permission of the author and the publisher.

cannot exclude the possibility that such groups had a specific meaning of their own, they may represent the 'asemic' sort of pseudo-script (see Section 4.2), expressing nothing but the suggestion of Egyptian writing: 'the "anra" formula did not have a consistent meaning but was rather treated as a generic group of good luck symbols with Egyptian prestige value'.[68]

---

[68] Ben-Tor 2009: 87, rejecting Fiona Richards' interpretation of the ⁽-n-r sequence as a writing of the West-Semitic name El ( '*l*) (Richards 2001: 150–60), as well as the ideographic interpretation 'giving an offering', 'water' and 'bread/cake' proposed by Orly Goldwasser (2006: 130–1). In both cases, the reason for rejection is the diversity in the selection and order of signs on the individual scarabs. It is not likely that hieroglyphic ⁽-n-r reflects Semitic '*l*; the one case of Egyptian ⁽ (*'ayin*) for Semitic ' (*'aleph*) listed by Hoch (1994: 431, referred to by Richards), when compared with the well-attested correspondences ⁽ (Semitic) – ⁽ (Egyptian) and ' (Semitic) – ꝫ or *j* (Egyptian), is 'rare and perhaps erroneous' (Hoch 1994: 386, 413 – attestation Nineteenth Dynasty!). It remains unclear, therefore, what inspired the selection of the three Egyptian hieroglyphs by the producers of Canaanite scarabs.

The Levantine scarabs show their own particular iconographic configurations, many of which testify to a limited understanding of Egyptian signs and sign groups that served as their examples. But the reinterpretation and reconfiguration of hieroglyphs, even into apparently meaningless groupings, was not restricted to producers living outside Egypt. Scarabs produced in Egypt during the Middle Kingdom and later also included creative regroupings of conventional signs, some of which seem to be free variations of regular or formal hieroglyphic compositions, and which could have served as examples for scarabs produced outside Egypt (Ben-Tor 2009: 94, figure 3). As mentioned earlier in this section, even earlier Egyptian stamp seals show pseudo-hieroglyphic groups, and thus testify to limited understanding but a creative use of hieroglyphs by their Egyptian makers and users.

## 5.2 Early Levantine Writing: Cuneiform and Hieroglyphic, the Byblos Script

Given the widespread use of Egyptian hieroglyphs on Egyptian and locally made artefacts in the Levant, it comes as no surprise that writing systems developed there were partly influenced by Egyptian writing. To be sure, Egyptian scripts (hieroglyphic and hieratic) were not the only sort of writing used in this region. From the late fourth millennium onward, Mesopotamian (proto-)writing was used there as well, especially in Syria. During the Late Bronze Age (*c*.1600–1200 BC), the use of clay tablets and cuneiform writing, in Akkadian and other languages, extended from Mesopotamia, Syria and Anatolia to the southern Levant and to Egypt (Van Soldt 2013). This led to at least one adaptation of cuneiform writing to a local language: that of the Syrian city state of Ugarit, where alphabetic (i.e. *abjad*) cuneiform writing developed by approximately 1300 BC. A list of alphabetic cuneiform characters found at Beth Shemesh to the west of Jerusalem shows that this writing system was not restricted to Ugarit, nor even to the northern Levant (Ferrara 2020: 25).

The southern Levant was politically dominated by Egypt throughout the Late Bronze Age, and scanty remains of hieratic text on pottery sherds testify to Egyptian written administration there (Wimmer 2008a). Papyri, which would have been mainly used for this purpose, are all lost. But the significant impact of administrative hieratic writing in the Levant is clear from much later ostraca on which Canaanite alphabetic writing is combined with numerical notation derived from hieratic (eighth to sixth centuries BC: Wimmer 2008b).

Hieroglyphic inscriptions incised on stone, metal, wood and ceramic surfaces, such as the scarabs discussed in the previous section, have survived much better. As in Egypt itself, the use of this script and the choice of materials were motivated by the commemorative and religious purposes of the texts. This is true for Egyptian imports, such as scarabs and inscribed stone vases (e.g. Montet 1928: 84–90), as well as for hieroglyphic texts made in the Levant. A prime example of the latter is the use of Egyptian hieroglyphs by the rulers of Byblos in a late phase of the Middle Bronze Age. Hieroglyphic inscriptions on stone monuments (e.g. Montet 1928: 90–3) and on precious objects found in the royal tombs (Kopetzky 2018) mention the kings buried there. The names are clearly local, written with phonograms only (e.g. ⌇⌇ *jn-n-t-n* for *Jntn* 'Yantin'), but the accompanying title, filiations and epithets show conventional Egyptian orthographies.[69] Byblos had important trade links with Egypt for centuries. Egyptian cultural influence was considerable, and Egyptian-style inscriptions, objects and architecture are especially well attested at Byblos for this period. For this reason, the appearance of a local pictorial script showing some resemblance to Egyptian hieroglyphs has traditionally been ascribed to the Middle Bronze Age.[70] This so-called Byblos script (less appropriately called 'pseudo-hieroglyphic') is known from fourteen inscriptions on stone and metal, most of them rather brief (Vita & Zamora 2018; see Figure 17). The script remains undeciphered and the precise number of different characters is difficult to establish, but there are well over 100, and many of them are pictorial (Dunand 1945: 88–115; Vita & Zamora 2018: 90–8). Their resemblance to Egyptian hieroglyphs is limited, however. Signs depicting human body parts (such as the eye or lower arm) and

**Figure 17** The Byblos script on a bronze tablet. After Dunand (1945: 75, figure 28).

---

[69] The Egyptian title the Byblos kings used is ⌇ *haty-a* (*ḥꜣty-ꜥ*). When used in Egypt, this title refers to mayors or provincial governors, but in Byblos, it does not seem to express a role akin to Egyptian administration. From an Egyptian perspective, the king of Byblos was called *ḥqꜣ* 'ruler', or *mꜣkj* (possibly a transcription of Semitic *mlk* 'king') in the late Twelfth Dynasty (Allen 2008: 33). In Mari, in the eighteenth century BC, the ruler of Byblos was called 'king' (*šarru*; see Guichard 2005: 461). The use of terms specifically associated with pharaonic kingship (such as *ny-swt*) was probably felt to be inappropriate in a non-Egyptian country.

[70] That dating has recently been challenged, on good grounds, by Benjamin Sass (2019), who points to a number of similarities, both in text layout and in the forms of some individual signs, with alphabetic writing of the early first millennium BC. Archaeological (i.e. stratigraphic) evidence for the dates of the inscriptions is too meagre to be of help.

animals (e.g. birds, snakes) are reminiscent of hieroglyphs, but may also represent concrete items without being hieroglyphs, and only a few signs have forms that appear typically Egyptian (e.g. the house plan ⌐⌐, the headrest ⋉). Several more have rather abstract geometric shapes. This last category has led to the idea that some of the signs are of hieratic inspiration (Posener 1969; Vita & Zamora 2018: 93).

The truth is probably that there is no one-to-one relationship between the Byblos script and any Egyptian script (monumental or cursive), and that the same applies to individual characters of these scripts. And in the absence of scholarly consensus about the meaning of the signs and the workings of the Byblos script, graphic resemblance to other writing systems (or the lack of it) is the single indication for the potential role of cross-cultural inspiration. It is interesting, however, to see that three graphic categories can possibly be distinguished in the Byblos sign repertoire: one directly inspired by specific Egyptian hieroglyphs, one consisting of pictorial signs not necessarily derived from specific hieroglyphs and one of abstract shapes and uncertain graphic motivation. All possible categories, and combinations of these, should be kept in mind when studying the Byblos characters, just as in the case of the Egyptian identity marks that were the topic of Section 4.2, and in the case of another Levantine script, which is the topic of the following section.

## 5.3 The Early *Abjad*

At some point in the second millennium BC appeared a writing system that is generally considered to be the oldest known precursor to all ancient and modern alphabets. Its most abundant attestation is a corpus of fifty inscriptions on rock surfaces and statuary at Serabit el-Khadim and its surroundings, in the south of the Sinai Peninsula. This script is commonly referred to as 'Proto-Sinaitic'.[71] Two minuscule inscriptions in what seems to be a very similar script have been discovered in the Wadi el-Hol, in the Western Desert of Egypt, to the northwest of Luxor (Darnell et al. 2005). The dating of the inscriptions at both sites is controversial, but most specialists consider the early second millennium (nineteenth–eighteenth centuries) BC to be the most likely period.[72] An even more

---

[71] There is a sea of literature on Proto-Sinaitic and related scripts. The most important collections of relevant material are Sass (1988) and Hamilton (2006), supplemented with more recently discovered texts by Tallet (2012). Recent, exhaustive documentation and discussion is given by Morenz (2019), with magnificent drawings by David Sabel. Otherwise, the main recent discussions are by Goldwasser (e.g. 2012, 2016, 2022).

[72] For example, Sass 1988: 141–4; Morenz 2011; Goldwasser 2012. Hamilton (2006: 295–303) proposed a longer time span during which the inscriptions were made, mainly 1850–1500 BC. This section is not the place for a lengthy discussion of the dates proposed; suffice it to say that these range between circa 1850 and 1300 BC. The youngest date was proposed by Sass (2005), after reconsidering the dating in Sass 1988; a date of circa 1600 BC has been proposed by Briquel-Chatonnet (1998). The discovery of an Egyptian ostracon of the fifteenth century BC

precise date assigned to both the Sinai and the Wadi el-Hol texts is the reign of Amenemhat III (Sass 1988: 142; Darnell et al. 2005: 90; Goldwasser 2012: 12; 2022: 15). The reason for such a precise date is the fact that local Egyptian hieroglyphic inscriptions of that reign testify to expeditions (mining expeditions in Serabit, military ones in the Wadi el-Hol) that include Levantine participants, even leaders. No clear connection exists between these inscriptions and the alphabetic ones, except possible palaeographic similarities (see later in this section), and the fact that they are found in the same area. Both locations were also visited in earlier and later periods, but mining at Serabit was especially intensive during the late Twelfth Dynasty, if the Egyptian inscriptions left there are anything to go by, and the combining of Egyptian and Levantine members within the same expeditions certainly seems an ideal background of using the alphabetic script of Serabit el-Khadim and Wadi el-Hol.[73]

Although the Proto-Sinaitic script has by no means been fully deciphered, several phrases have been successfully identified, some of these already in the early twentieth century, most importantly by Alan Gardiner (1916). Two phrases recurring in different texts are *lb 'lt* 'for the Mistress' and *mh(b)b 'lt* 'beloved of the Mistress' (Figure 18). The interpretation of the individual characters is based on several mutually supportive assumptions: (1) the script serves to express a West-Semitic language closely related to (but antedating) Biblical Hebrew and related languages; (2) the notions depicted by the Proto-Sinaitic signs (e.g. house, water, eye) are to be connected with the names of the Hebrew letters in Biblical tradition (e.g. *bēt* 'house', *mēm* 'water', *'ayin* 'eye'); (3) the sounds expressed by the signs are the first sounds of these names (*b, m, '*); (4) the signs are graphic precursors of the earliest Hebrew, Phoenician and Aramaic linear characters (as is particularly clear for some of the signs, e.g. *mēm, 'ayin, tau*). Assumptions (2) and (3) are the most important keys to the understanding of the Proto-Sinaitic script: the signs stand for single consonants derived by acrophony from the names of the

---

that shows part of the so-called *halaḥam* alphabetic sequence, as well as several signs closely resembling those of Serabit and Wadi el-Hol (Haring 2015c), indicates that the *invention* of the script took place before the mid-second millennium.

[73] See Parker 2022 for a recent assessment of the archaeological evidence: stylistic dating of the inscribed objects, distribution of Proto-Sinaitic inscriptions and their possible relations with Egyptian inscriptions and architecture. The rough style of royal and private statuary bearing Proto-Sinaitic texts (and indeed that of Serabit statuary in general) makes dating on stylistic grounds difficult, and it cannot be excluded that Proto-Sinaitic texts on Egyptian-style objects and near Egyptian rock inscriptions were added later (probably with the exception of block statue Cairo JE 38268 and busts Brussels E. 2428–9, apparently made to receive their proto-Sinaitic inscriptions, but also the most difficult of all to connect with datable Egyptian style; see Parker 2022: 279–83). It seems to me that no individual Proto-Sinaitic inscription can be dated to the late Twelfth Dynasty with certainty, but the entire package of evidence – that is, the distribution of the inscriptions and their possible relations to Egyptian(-style) objects and inscriptions – does make such a dating very plausible.

**Figure 18** Proto-Sinaitic inscription: *mh(b)b'lt* 'beloved of the Mistress.' From Hamilton (2006: 332, figure A.7 top); reproduced here with kind permission of the publisher.

notions depicted. Since the script is supposed to reflect consonants only, it should be referred to as *abjad*, rather than alphabet (see Section 2.3).

The validity of this explanatory model is supported by the sequences deciphered so far – although these are few. The phrases *lb'lt* 'for the Mistress' and *mh(b)b'lt* 'beloved of the Mistress' appear to be votive formulae, as can be expected on objects deposited in a temple, and in textual graffiti. The 'Mistress' is thought to refer to the deity worshipped in the temple at Serabit, who is probably to be identified with the goddess Hathor mentioned in the local Egyptian texts. One of the objects found in this temple, a small sandstone sphinx now in the British Museum, has both phrases on its base (Figure 18).[74] The same sphinx bears two Egyptian hieroglyphic inscriptions: one (almost entirely lost) between the front legs mentioning the name of the royal figure represented by the sphinx, and one (better preserved) that says, 'beloved of Hathor, [Mistress of] Turquoise'. 'Mistress of Turquoise' (*nbt mfk3t*) is the usual epithet in Egyptian texts of the goddess as she was worshipped at Serabit, turquoise being the chief object of local mining activities. The Egyptian text on the sphinx is clearly similar in meaning to the hypothetical reading of the Proto-Sinaitic text on the same object as *mh(b)b'lt* 'beloved of the Mistress', and thus supports that reading. There are some other sequences in Proto-Sinaitic inscriptions that are more or less

---

[74] BM EA 41748 = Sinai 345, most recently discussed together with the other inscribed objects from the temple by Goldwasser (2022). Previous discussions are by Sass (1988: 12–14), Hamilton (2006: 332–5) and Morenz (2019: 196–204).

commonly accepted, such as the title *rb nqbn* 'chief of miners', but there is little consensus about the meaning of the longer texts, and also the Wadi el-Hol inscriptions still await convincing interpretation.[75]

Acrophony is central to the understanding of Proto-Sinaitic, and so it must have been to the inventors of this writing system. More precisely, the selection of the initial consonants of words expressing the notions depicted by Proto-Sinaitic characters is a clear case of 'strong' acrophony as described by Pascal Vernus (2015; see Section 2.3). 'Weak' acrophony, in which monosyllabic words are reduced to one consonant by losing their 'weak' ending (often a mere vowel), can be a natural linguistic process, whereas 'strong' acrophony, in which a longer string of sounds following the initial one is dropped, is a conscious choice of language and script users (Vernus 2015: 160). It follows that the development of the writing system underlying the Proto-Sinaitic inscriptions was a consistently planned process.

Orly Goldwasser (2006: 132–3; 2012) and Ludwig Morenz (2011: 223–42; 2019: 273) have argued repeatedly that Serabit was the place where the Proto-Sinaitic *abjad* was invented. One reason for this is the cooperation between Egyptians and Levantines as documented by Egyptian hieroglyphic texts of the late Twelfth Dynasty at Serabit, as mentioned earlier in this section. Additional support is seen by Goldwasser (2006: 135–51) and Morenz (2011: 134–7) in palaeographic similarities between Proto-Sinaitic characters and Twelfth Dynasty hieroglyphs at the site. Although the Wadi el-Hol inscriptions are dated to the same period as the Proto-Sinaitic ones by their discoverers, the palaeography of individual Wadi el-Hol characters are linked by them to earlier monumental and cursive Egyptian signs, thus betraying an origin of the script in the early- to mid-Twelfth Dynasty (Darnell et al. 2005: 90). Two critical thoughts about these datings may be given a priori: (1) The very small corpus of *abjad* inscriptions in the Sinai and the Wadi el-Hol is an insecure basis for palaeographic analysis; (2) if the same script is attested at two sites lying far from each other, and if it was indeed applied in both places at about the same time, it seems more likely that by that time, the use of the script in question had already spread over a wide area and the date of its invention was older (Haring 2020: 57).

Goldwasser more specifically argues that the Proto-Sinaitic script was invented by illiterate miners working at the turquoise mines around Serabit el-Khadim, during or before the reign of Amenemhat III. Reacting to a 2010 blog

---

[75] No translation of the Wadi el-Hol texts was suggested by Darnell et al. (2005: 85–6). Interpretations of many Proto-Sinaitic texts were given by Albright (1948), but these have not met with consensus in subsequent scholarship. Compare more recent interpretations in Sass 1988 and Wilson-Wright 2013 and 2020.

by Christopher Rollston[76], in whose opinion the inventors were rather to be sought within Canaanite elite circles who were in close contact with Egyptians, Goldwasser referred to the crude style of Proto-Sinaitic texts at Serabit as an indication for the makers' inability to read Egyptian hieroglyphs (Goldwasser 2012). To this one may agree in the sense that it would not have been necessary for the makers of the Proto-Sinaitic inscriptions we see today to understand Egyptian hieroglyphs. Whether the same was true for the *inventors* of the script they were using is a different matter. The Proto-Sinaitic script has important characteristics in common with Egyptian hieroglyphic: not only does it have pictorial signs, but it also reduces written language to consonants, written with mono-consonantal signs, the phonetic values of which were determined by acrophony. It may be suggested, therefore, that the inventors had some degree of familiarity with Egyptian writing, however superficial. 'Semi-literacy' seems a more appropriate term in this context than 'illiteracy', as the latter implies total ignorance of the principles of writing. As we have seen in the section on marks and pseudo-script (Section 4.2), the notion of semi-literacy includes many sorts of reading and writing skills; in fact, semi-literacy can be everything between (but different from) illiteracy on the one hand and full literacy on the other.

The inventors of the writing system behind the Proto-Sinaitic and Wadi el-Hol inscriptions were thus *at least* semi-literate,[77] and probably developed the system some time before its application in Sinai and Wadi el-Hol. As we have seen, an earlier dating of the latter was also proposed, on palaeographic grounds, by Darnell et al. (2015). If that is indeed the case, the Sinai and Wadi el-Hol characters may be seen as crude ad hoc specimens of signs of an already existing writing system, and their resemblance, in the Sinai, to signs of local hieroglyphic Twelfth Dynasty inscriptions could mean nothing more than that the latter were a source of inspiration for the *style* of the Proto-Sinaitic characters as made at the same site.

The inventors of the earliest documented *abjad*, elite or not, likely had some knowledge of Egyptian hieroglyphic writing. Regular hieroglyphic orthography (i.e. combinations of ideograms and mono-, bi- and triconsonantal phonograms), which was so much connected with Egyptian linguistic and cultural notions, would have been difficult to use for words of a non-Egyptian language.

---

[76] ASOR Blog: https://asorblog.org/?p=427, although the 2010 blog by Rollston could no longer be retrieved at the time of writing this Element. His argument proceeded from (1) the contention that literacy (alphabetic or not) in antiquity was typically an elite feature; (2) the observation that members of the Canaanite elite were present at Serabit, and were the authors of some of the local Egyptian hieroglyphic inscriptions.

[77] An additional argument against the total illiteracy of the inventors is the very analysis of language as a string of sounds (or phonemes), rather than syllables, which is considered typical for literate speakers; see Section 2.3.

Mono-consonantal phonograms were the obvious choice for this, *being precisely the choice the Egyptian scribes made for the same purpose*. One might object that the inventors, if familiar with Egyptian writing, could have adopted the existing set of Egyptian mono-consonantal hieroglyphs (as indeed suggested by Briquel-Chatonnet 1998: 58; Goldwasser 2012: 14).[78] Signs possibly derived from these hieroglyphs are rare in the Proto-Sinaitic texts, and those we might want to identify as such (with ⌐⌐, ⌐, ⌐ and ⌐ as conceivable hieroglyphic prototypes) have phonetic values different from the Egyptian ones (*y*, *n*, *m* and *ḥ* respectively, according to current interpretations, instead of the expected *ꜥ*, *ḏ*, *n* and *ḥ*). The question of why the inventors would have (partially) deviated from Egyptian graphic and conceptual models is difficult to answer since we know next to nothing about their cultural and social background. We do not know when and where they lived, or precisely what linguistic and cultural factors determined the new script.[79] The crude forms of the Proto-Sinaitic and Wadi el-Hol signs make it difficult to connect them with specific Egyptian hieroglyphs except in a very few cases,[80] and for some of the signs, no hieroglyphic prototypes present themselves at all.

The *abjad* users in the southern Sinai may have been far removed, both chronologically and geographically, from the script's origins, as is shown by the often divergent orientations of text and of individual signs and the palaeographic appearance and stances of these signs, although there are differences in quality even within the extremely limited Proto-Sinaitic corpus.[81] Egyptian

---

[78] Compare the case of Meroitic hieroglyphs at the beginning of Section 5; of the twenty-three characters of the Meroitic alphasyllabary, many seem to have derived their phonetic value from their Egyptian prototypes, although changing these from consonantal signs to syllables or vowels. Note, however, that very few of the borrowed signs express single consonants in Egyptian; some are in fact originally biconsonantal signs, or even ideograms.

[79] Briquel-Chatonnet (1998: 59–60) considered this argument, previously given by Romain Butin, a cheap one; unjustly so in my opinion. Adaptations and replacements are to be expected in the development of new scripts inspired by existing ones. The Meroitic alphasyllabary did not simply take over the Egyptian mono-consonantal 'set' (see the previous footnote). According to Morenz (2009), the Proto-Sinaitic sign repertoire is a reflection of the inventors' world view. A recent and excellent approach by Nadia Ben-Marzouk (2022) regards the early pictorial alphabet as a conscious mixture of Egyptian and non-Egyptian features, 'othering' the new script from its Egyptian inspiration, and thus instrumental in strengthening the group identity of its inventors. A deliberate departure from Egyptian sign orientation was already considered by Hamilton (2006: 282).

[80] A stronger case than the hieroglyphs mentioned in this paragraph is the hieroglyphic equivalent of the man with raised arms (used for /h/ in Proto-Sinaitic), which is frequent in Egyptian inscriptions at Serabit (Goldwasser 2006: 137–8), but this particular case stands alone. One of the Sinai forms of *bet* 'house', a rectangle with or without an opening in one of the sides or corners, is also found on hieroglyphic stela Sinai 92; Goldwasser (2012: 17–18) argued that the borrowing there went in the reverse direction – that is, from Proto-Sinaitic to Egyptian.

[81] Some inscriptions at mine L look more standardized and 'scribal' than the other texts: they have straight horizontal lines with framing borders, and the orientation of their signs is more consistent (Goldwasser 2022: 25–9).

hieroglyphs may have been the initial graphic models for some of the signs, but these subsequently went through a process similar to the identity marks of Deir el-Medina workmen (see Section 4.2). A mark originally inspired by a hieroglyphic or hieratic falcon became a birdlike sign that was in no way reminiscent of a falcon, and a mark depicting a jar could be rendered with or without handles or liquid issuing from it. In her discussions of the development of alphabetic writing in the Levant *after* the invention of Proto-Sinaitic, Goldwasser (2016) saw the same process and demonstrated that the individual signs were distinctive without being graphically precise. Not the precise shapes of characters, but the recognizability of the notions represented ('recognition cues') was central in the Levantine alphabet until approximately 1300 BC, when a more standardized linear, non-pictorial script developed (Goldwasser 2016). In this sense, characters of the earliest Levantine *abjad*s were 'concrete' referents, just like the Deir el-Medina marks. Many of the latter derived from hieroglyphs but became graphically detached from them, and were not subjected to palaeographic standardization for several centuries, even within the same small community of users. Yet these users were not entirely illiterate, and the same is probably true for the inventors of the Proto-Sinaitic script.

# 6 Conclusion

In the preceding sections, the reader, travelling from specialist to hyper-specialist to less-than-specialist applications of hieroglyphs, has come to know Egyptian hieroglyphic writing as an extremely versatile script that enabled multiple ways of producing and understanding monumental inscriptions. Hieroglyphs were also the source of inspiration for different sorts of emblems, marks, pseudo-scripts and newly invented writing systems for non-Egyptian languages. It is clear that Egyptian hieroglyphs enjoyed a high degree of cultural prestige and visual appeal to an Egyptian audience as well as to foreign ones. To be sure, this prestige and appeal was not enjoyed by hieroglyphs only, but also by other Egyptian scripts (hieratic and Demotic), by Egyptian visual expression and by pharaonic elite culture in a broad sense. But the hieroglyphic script had something particularly special to offer. It presented a vast repertoire of pictorial signs, including culturally powerful icons, with infinite potential for linguistic and non-linguistic expression. Only part of that potential could be touched upon in this Element, the text of which is limited to the discussions of a few selected examples and case studies

Diverse as the examples presented might be, some important central issues surfaced in several of the cases discussed. They are all about the inspiration and creativity of different groups or individuals who used hieroglyphs for their own specific purposes. In many cases, the inspiration was linguistic as much as it was visual. Scripts inspired by regular hieroglyphic texts, such as enigmatic Egyptian writing, but also the Meroitic syllabary and the Levantine *abjad*, were based on phonetic modification (including, but not restricted to, acrophony), which enabled scribes to incorporate individual characters into unusual orthographies, or to adapt them for the notation of non-Egyptian languages. For the latter purpose, phonetic modification was combined with graphic changes, first of all with the reduction to a very limited repertoire of signs. The individual signs of these limited sign-sets could follow Egyptian models more or less precisely, as in the case of Meroitic, but could also deviate considerably from them in the case of the earliest Levantine *abjad*. Indeed, it is to be doubted if the characters of this Levantine script, the earliest known precursor to modern alphabetic writing, had any direct relation with individual Egyptian hieroglyphs. Although some of the individual *abjad* characters might have hieroglyphic origins, the inspiration felt by the inventors of the new script seems to have been mainly conceptual. Its most important similarity to Egyptian writing is the very use of pictorial signs to express single consonants.

Mono-consonantal writing is a more important feature of Egyptian scripts than one might realize when reading 'regular' hieroglyphic texts. Although writing entire words with signs for single consonants was less usual after the Old Kingdom than it had been in earlier centuries, it resurfaced whenever scribes deviated from regular hieroglyphic orthography. Hieroglyphic specialists felt the need to do this when writing foreign words and names, or even new words in their own language, for which no classical Egyptian spellings presented themselves. They also resorted to single consonants in the hyper-specialist applications that were enigmatic and Ptolemaic writing. Even funerary inscriptions made by less knowledgeable Egyptian artists occasionally include unusual mono-consonantal spellings, indicating an insufficient mastering of conventional orthography. It is conceivable that writing single consonants as a strategy existed as a subsystem in the minds of professional scribes as well as semi-literates, and surfaced whenever the writing job at hand was out of the ordinary, and the restraints of regular hieroglyphic orthography lessened. This was the 'alphabetic consciousness' Alan Gardiner saw in the abbreviations of names to single hieroglyphs (Gardiner 1947: 12; see Section 2.3). Such a strategy possibly also inspired the inventors of new scripts for non-Egyptian languages.[82] It was typical for the hieroglyphic script, in which individual signs were discrete (that is, not graphically joined), and different orthographies were

---

[82] As already suggested by Jean François Champollion in his *Lettre à M. Dacier* of 1822; see Laboury 2022b: 66.

used for the same words. Hieratic and Demotic also included signs and sign groups for single consonants, but writing and reading these scripts depended more on graphically joined groups of signs and on the orthography of complete words, whereas hieroglyphs presented more possibilities for sign-by-sign interpretation.

Hieroglyphic inspiration was certainly not restricted to linguistic applications. The use of hieroglyphs as emblems in visual and sculptural compositions demonstrates that these signs, although components of a writing system, and as such being signs of double articulation, could also function without their syntactic role and become signs of single articulation, conveying their messages by themselves. This is perhaps no surprise in the case of logograms or radicograms that express important religious or practical notions, such as $\bar{\varphi}$ 'life', $\mathscr{A}$ 'Horus' and $\bar{\varrho}$ 'good', especially in royal, funerary and administrative contexts – the domains of elite society and culture. In these contexts, the meaning and graphic shape of the signs remained close to those in hieroglyphic texts. One step further was the use of the same signs as signifiers of non-elite persons, such as workmen or teams of workmen. Although the meaning of such identity marks as hieroglyphs remained relevant in many cases, as references to the names of individuals, institutions or places, they were effectively taken out of the writing system they were originally part of, became signs of single articulation and played a role in marking systems that included signs of different graphic categories: abstract geometric signs and pictorial but non-hieroglyphic signs. From that point onward, their precise hieroglyphic shape had less relevance, as long as they were mutually distinctive, and could be recognized as references to their users.

As adaptable characters of Egyptian writing systems, as individual emblems and as components of new scripts and notations, hieroglyphs offered truly endless possibilities.

# References

Abd El-Sattar, I. (2021). Remarks on the orthography of word *rmṯ* in the Old Kingdom. *Zeitschrift für ägyptische Sprache und Altertumskunde*, 148, 1–11.

Albright, W. F. (1948). The early alphabetic inscriptions from Sinai and their decipherment. *Bulletin of the American Schools of Oriental Research*, 110, 6–22.

Allen, J. (2008). The historical inscription of Khnumhotep at Dahshur: preliminary report. *Bulletin of the American Schools of Oriental Research*, 352, 29–39.

Allen, J. (2014). *Middle Egyptian: An Introduction to the Language and Culture of Hieroglyphs*. 3rd ed. Cambridge: Cambridge University Press.

Allen, J. (2020). *Ancient Egyptian Phonology*. Cambridge: Cambridge University Press.

Andrássy, P. (2009a). Dic Teammarken der Bauleute des ägyptischen Alten und Mittleren Reiches. In B. Haring & O. Kaper, eds., *Pictograms or Pseudo Script? Non-textual Identity Marks in Practical Use in Ancient Egypt and Elsewhere: Proceedings of a Conference in Leiden, 19–20 December 2006*. Leiden: Nederlands Instituut voor het Nabije Oosten and Peeters, pp. 5–48.

Andrássy, P. (2009b). Symbols in the Reisner papyri. In P. Andrássy, J. Budka & F. Kammerzell, eds., *Non-textual Marking Systems, Writing and Pseudo Script from Prehistory to Modern Times*. Gottingen: Seminar für Ägyptologie und Koptologie, pp. 113–22.

Andrássy, P., Budka, J. & Kammerzell, F., eds. (2009). *Non-textual Marking Systems, Writing and Pseudo Script from Prehistory to Modern Times*. Gottingen: Seminar für Ägyptologie und Koptologie.

Andreu-Lanoë, G. & Valbelle, D. (2022). *Guide de Deir el-Médina*. Cairo: Institut Français d'Archéologie Orientale.

Bács, T. A. (2011). '... Like heaven in its interior': late Ramesside painters in Theban Tomb 65. In Z. A. Hawass, T. A. Bács & G. Schreiber, eds., *Proceedings of the Colloquium on Theban Archaeology at the Supreme Council of Antiquities, November 5, 2009*. Cairo: Supreme Council of Antiquities, pp. 33–41.

Baines, J. (2004). The earliest Egyptian writing: development, context, purpose. In S. Houston, ed., *The First Writing: Script Invention As History and Process*. Cambridge: Cambridge University Press, pp. 150–89.

Baines, J. (2007). Communication and display: the integration of early Egyptian art and writing. In J. Baines, ed., *Visual and Written Culture in Ancient Egypt*. Oxford: Oxford University Press, pp. 281–97.

Baines, J. & Eyre, C. (2007). Four notes on literacy. In J. Baines, ed., *Visual and Written Culture in Ancient Egypt*. Oxford: Oxford University Press, pp. 63–94, 172–4.

Ben-Marzouk, N. (2022). Othering the alphabet: rewriting the social context of a new writing system in the Egyptian expedition community. In D. Candelora, N. Ben-Marzouk & K. Cooney, eds., *Ancient Egyptian Society: Challenging Assumptions, Exploring Approaches*. London: Routledge, pp. 279–98.

Ben-Tor, D. (2007). *Scarabs, Chronology, and Interconnections: Egypt and Palestine in the Second Intermediate Period*. Fribourg: Academic Press and Vandenhoeck & Ruprecht.

Ben-Tor, D. (2009). Pseudo hieroglyphs on Middle Bronze Age Canaanite scarabs. In P. Andrássy, J. Budka & F. Kammerzell, eds., *Non-textual Marking Systems, Writing and Pseudo Script from Prehistory to Modern Times*. Gottingen: Seminar für Ägyptologie und Koptologie, pp. 83–100.

Bierbrier, M. (1982). *The Tomb-Builders of the Pharaohs*. London: British Museum Publications.

Boardman, J. (2010). Seals and signs: Anatolian stamp seals of the Persian period revisited. In J. Evans Pim, S. A. Yatsenko & O. T. Perrin, eds., *Traditional Marking Systems: A Preliminary Survey*. Dover: Dunkling Books, pp. 153–80.

Boas, G. (1993). *The Hieroglyphics of Horapollo*. 2nd ed. Princeton, NJ: Princeton University Press.

Boot, E. (2005). *Continuity and Change in Text and Image at Chichén Itzá, Yucatán, Mexico*. Leiden: CNWS Publications.

Boud'hors, A., Dixneuf, D., Guermeur, I. et al. (2021). Les dépotoirs à tessons de Hout-Répit/Athribis et leur matériel inscrit. Rapport préliminaire (mission 2019–20). *Bulletin de l'Institut français d'archéologie orientale*, 121, 69–145.

Bréand, G. (2015). Pot marks on bread moulds in settlement context during Naqada III period. In J. Budka, F. Kammerzell & S. Rzepka, eds., *Non-textual Marking Systems in Ancient Egypt (and Elsewhere)*. Hamburg: Widmaier, pp. 187–213.

Bresciani, E. (1996). *Il volto di Osiri: tele funerarie dipinte nell'Egitto romano*. Lucca: Maria Pacini Fazzi Editore.

Briquel-Chatonnet, F. (1998). Les inscriptions proto-sinaïtiques. In D. Valbelle & C. Bonnet, eds., *Le Sinaï durant l'Antiquité et le Moyen Age*. Paris: Errance, pp. 56–60.

Bruyère, B. (1953). *Rapport sur les fouilles de Deir el Médineh (années 1948 à 1951)*. Cairo: Institut Français d'Archéologie Orientale.

Budge, E. A. W. (1923). *Facsimiles of Egyptian Hieratic Papyri in the British Museum*. Second series. London: Trustees of the British Museum.

Budka, J., Kammerzell, F. & Rzepka, S., eds. (2015). *Non-textual Marking Systems in Ancient Egypt (and Elsewhere)*. Hamburg: Widmaier.

Cabrol, A. (1995). Les criosphinx de Karnak: un nouveau dromos d'Amenhotep III. *Cahiers de Karnak*, 10, 1–28.

Cannuyer, C. (2018). Aux origines de l'ère copte dite 'des Martyrs' ou 'de Dioclétien': À propos d'une note de l'érudit protestant Johannes Nicolai. *Cahiers d'Égypte Nilotique et Mediterranéenne*, 19, 73–100.

Cauville, S. (1990). Les inscriptions dédicatoires du temple d'Hathor à Dendera. *Bulletin de l'Institut français d'archéologie orientale* 90, 83–114.

Cauville, S. (2002). Entre exigence décorative et significations multiples: les graphies suggestives du temple d'Hathor à Dendera. *Bulletin de l'Institut français d'archéologie orientale* 102, 91–135.

Černý, J. (2001). *A Community of Workmen at Thebes in the Ramesside Period*. 2nd ed. Cairo: Institut Français d'Archéologie Orientale.

Cherpion, N. (1999). *Deux tombes de la XVIIIe dynastie à Deir el-Medina: nos 340 (Amenemhat) et 354 (anonyme)*. Cairo: Institut Français d'Archéologie Orientale.

Collombert, P. (2007). Combien y avait-il de hiéroglyphes? *Égypte, Afrique & Orient*, 46, 15–28.

Cooney, K. M. (2007). *The Cost of Death: The Social and Economic Value of Ancient Egyptian Funerary Art in the Ramesside Period*. Leiden: Nederlands Instituut voor het Nabije Oosten.

Cooney, K. M. (2021). *Coffin Commerce: How a Funerary Materiality Formed Ancient Egypt*. Cambridge: Cambridge University Press.

Daniels, P. (2018). *An Exploration of Writing*. Sheffield: Equinox.

Daressy, G. (1902). *Fouilles de la Vallée des Rois*. Cairo: Institut Français d'Archéologie Orientale.

Darnell, J. C. (2017). The early hieroglyphic inscription at El-Khawy. *Archéo-Nil* 27, 49–64.

Darnell, J. C. (2020). Ancient Egyptian cryptography: graphic hermeneutics. In D. Klotz & A. Stauder, eds., *Enigmatic Writing in the New Kingdom I: Revealing, Transforming, and Display in Egyptian Hieroglyphs*. Berlin: De Gruyter, pp. 7–48.

Darnell, J. C., Dobbs-Allsopp, F. W., Lundberg, M. J. et al. (2005). Two early alphabetic inscriptions from the Wadi el-Ḥôl: new evidence for the origin of the alphabet from the Western Desert of Egypt. *Annual of the American Schools of Oriental Research* 59, 63–124.

Daumas, F. (1988–95). *Valeurs phonétiques des signes hiéroglyphiques d'époque gréco-romaine*. 4 vols. Montpellier: Université de Montpellier.

Davidson, A. (2019). Writing: the re-construction of language. *Language Sciences*, 72, 134–49.

Davies, B. G. (1999). *Who's Who at Deir el-Medina: A Prosopographic Study of the Royal Workmen's Community*. Leiden: Nederlands Instituut voor het Nabije Oosten.

Davies, B. G. (2018). *Life within the Five Walls: A Handbook to Deir el-Medina*. Wallasey: Abercromby Press.

De Buck, A. (1935). *The Egyptian Coffin Texts I: Texts of Spells 1–75*. Chicago, IL: University of Chicago Press.

Depauw, M. (2009). The semiotics of quarry marks applied to Late Period and Graeco-Roman Egypt. In P. Andrássy, J. Budka & F. Kammerzell, eds., *Non-textual Marking Systems, Writing and Pseudo Script from Prehistory to Modern Times*. Gottingen: Seminar für Ägyptologie und Koptologie, pp. 205–13.

Der Manuelian, P. (1994). *Living in the Past: Studies in Archaism of the Egyptian Twenty-Sixth Dynasty*. London: Kegan Paul International.

Devauchelle, D. (1994). 24 août 394–24 août 1994. 1600 ans. *Bulletin de la Société Française d'Égyptologie*, 131, 16–18.

Ditze, B. (2007). Gedrückt – Geritzt – Gekratzt. Die Gefäße mit Topfmarken. In E. B. Pusch, ed., *Die Keramik des Grabungsplatzes Q I Teil 2*. Hildesheim: Gerstenberg, pp. 269–507.

Donker van Heel, K. (2022). Le hiératique anormal. In S. Polis, ed., *Guide des écritures de l'Égypte ancienne*. Cairo: Institut Français d'Archéologie Orientale, pp. 70–1.

Dreyer, G. (1998). *Umm el-Qaab I: Das prädynstische Königsgrab U-j und seine frühen Schriftzeugnisse*. Mainz: Philipp von Zabern.

Dunand, M. (1945). *Byblia Grammata: documents et recherches sur le développement de l'écriture en Phénicie*. Beirut: République libanaise, Ministère de l'éducation nationale et des beaux-arts, Direction des antiquités.

Edel, A. (1955–64). *Altägyptische Grammatik*. 2 vols. Rome: Pontificium Institutum Biblicum.

El-Daly, O. (2005). *Egyptology: The Missing Millennium. Ancient Egypt in Medieval Arabic Writings*. London: UCL Press.

Elkins, J. (1999). *The Domain of Images*. Ithaca, NY: Cornell University Press.

Evans Pim, J., Yatsenko, S. A. & Perrin, O. T., eds. (2010). *Traditional Marking Systems: A Preliminary Survey*. Dover: Dunkling Books.

Ferrara, S. (2020). A 'top-down' re-invention of an old form: cuneiform alphabets in context. In Ph. Boyes and Ph. Steele, eds., *Understanding Relations between Scripts II: Early Alphabets*. Oxford: Oxbow Books, pp. 15–28.

Ferraris, E. (2022). TT8 Project: an introduction. In S. Töpfer, P. del Vesco & F. Poole, eds., *Deir el-Medina through the Kaleidoscope: Proceedings of the International Workshop Turin 8th–10th October 2018*. Medina: Franco Cosimo Panini Editore S.p.A., https://formazioneericerca.museoegizio.it/en/pubblicazioni/deir-el-medina-en, pp. 599–619.

Fischer, H. G. (1979). Archaeological aspects of epigraphy and palaeography. In R. Caminos & H. G. Fischer, eds., *Ancient Egyptian Epigraphy and Palaeography*. 2nd ed. New York: Metropolitan Museum of Art, pp. 27–50.

Fournet, J.-L. (2021). Horapollon: un hiéroglyphe encore à déchiffrer ou La question horapollinienne. In J.-L. Fournet, ed., *Les Hieroglyphica d'Horapollon de l'Égypte antique à l'Europe moderne. Histoire, fiction et réappropriation*. Paris: Association des Amis du Centre d'Histoire et Civilisation de Byzance, pp. 87–109.

Fronczak, M. & Rzepka, S. (2009). 'Funny signs' in Theban rock graffiti. In P. Andrássy, J. Budka & F. Kammerzell, eds., *Non-textual Marking Systems, Writing and Pseudo Script from Prehistory to Modern Times*. Gottingen: Seminar für Ägyptologie und Koptologie, pp. 159–78.

Gabler, K. (2018). *Who's Who around Deir el-Medina: Untersuchungen zur Organisation, Prosopographie und Entwicklung des Versorgungspersonals für die Arbeitersiedlung und das Tal der Könige*. Leiden: Nederlands Instituut voor het Nabije Oosten and Peeters.

Gallorini, C. (2009). Incised marks on pottery and other objects from Kahun. In B. Haring & O. Kaper, eds., *Pictograms or Pseudo Script? Non-textual Identity Marks in Practical Use in Ancient Egypt and Elsewhere: Proceedings of a Conference in Leiden, 19–20 December 2006*. Leiden: Nederlands Instituut voor het Nabije Oosten and Peeters, pp. 107–42.

Gardiner, A. (1916). The Egyptian origin of the Semitic alphabet. *Journal of Egyptian Archaeology*, 3, 1–16.

Gardiner, A. (1931). *The Library of A. Chester Beatty: Description of a Hieratic Papyrus with a Mythological Story, Love-Songs, and other Miscellaneous Texts*. London: Oxford University Press.

Gardiner, A. (1947). *Ancient Egyptian Onomastica*. 3 vols. London: Oxford University Press.

Gardiner, A. (1957). *Egyptian Grammar: Being an Introduction to the Study of Hieroglyphs*. 3rd ed. Oxford: Griffith Institute.

Gelb, I. (1952). *A Study of Writing: The Foundations of Grammatology*. London: Routledge and Kegan Paul.

Goldwasser, O. (2002). *Prophets, Lovers and Giraffes: Wor(l)d Classification in Ancient Egypt*. Wiesbaden: Harrassowitz.

Goldwasser, O. (2006). Canaanites reading hieroglyphs: Horus is Hathor? The invention of the alphabet in Sinai. *Ägypten und Levante*, 16, 121–60.

Goldwasser, O. (2012). The miners who invented the alphabet: a response to Christopher Rollston. *Journal of Ancient Egyptian Interconnections*, 4, 9–22.

Goldwasser, O. (2016). From the iconic to the linear: the Egyptian scribes of Lachish and the modification of the early alphabet in the Late Bronze Age. In I. Finkelstein, I. Robin & T. Römer, eds., *Alphabets, Texts and Artifacts in the Ancient Near East: Studies Presented to Benjamin Sass*. Paris: Van Dieren, pp. 118–60.

Goldwasser, O. (2022). The early alphabetic inscriptions found by the shrine of Hathor at Serabit el-Khadem: palaeography, materiality, and agency. *Israel Exploration Journal*, 72, 14–48.

Grandet, P. (2022). Le hiératique. In S. Polis, ed., *Guide des écritures de l'Égypte ancienne*. Cairo: Institut Français d'Archéologie Orientale, pp. 62–9.

Griffith, F. L. (1889). *The Inscriptions of Siûṭ and Dêr Rîfeh*. London: Trübner and Company.

Griffith, F. L. (1911). *Meroitic Inscriptions I*. London: Egypt Exploration Fund.

Griffith, F. L. (1935–7). *Catalogue of the Demotic Graffiti of the Dodecaschoenus*. 2 vols. Oxford: Oxford University Press.

Grimal, N., Hallof, J. & Van der Plas, D. (2000). *Hieroglyphica. Sign list – Liste des signes – Zeichenliste*. 2nd ed. Utrecht: Centre for Computer-Aided Egyptological Research.

Guichard, M. (2005). *La vaiselle de luxe des rois de Mari*. Paris: Éditions Recherche sur les Civilisations.

Hamilton, G. (2006). *The Origins of the West Semitic Alphabet in Egyptian Scripts*. Washington, DC: Catholic Biblical Association of America.

Haring, B. (2000). Towards decoding the necropolis workmen's funny signs. *Göttinger Miszellen*, 178, 45–58.

Haring, B. (2003). From oral practice to written record in Ramesside Deir el-Medina. *Journal of the Economic and Social History of the Orient*, 46, 249–72.

Haring, B. (2006). Scribes and scribal activity at Deir el-Medina. In A. Dorn & T. Hofmann, eds., *Living and Writing in Deir el-Medina: Socio-historical Embodiment of Deir el-Medine Texts*. Basel: Schwabe, pp. 107–12.

Haring, B. (2009). On the nature of the workmen's marks of the royal necropolis administration in the New Kingdom. In P. Andrássy, J. Budka & F. Kammerzell, eds., *Non-textual Marking Systems, Writing and Pseudo Script from Prehistory to Modern Times*. Gottingen: Seminar für Ägyptologie und Koptologie, pp. 123–35.

Haring, B. (2010). Nineteenth Dynasty stelae and the merits of hieroglyphic palaeography. *Bibliotheca Orientalis*, 67, 22–34.

Haring, B. (2015a). Hieratic drafts for hieroglyphic texts? In U. Verhoeven, ed., *Ägyptologische 'Binsen'-Weisheiten I–II: Neue Forschungen und Methoden der Hieratistik. Akten zweier Tagungen in Mainz im April 2011 und März 2013*. Mainz: Akademie der Wissenschaften und der Literatur and Franz Steiner, pp. 67–84.

Haring, B. (2015b). Between administrative writing and work practice: marks ostraca and the roster of day duties of the royal necropolis workmen in the New Kingdom. In J. Budka, F. Kammerzell & S. Rzepka, eds., *Non-textual Marking Systems in Ancient Egypt (and Elsewhere)*. Hamburg: Widmaier, pp. 133–42.

Haring, B. (2015c). Halaḥam on an ostracon of the Early New Kingdom? *Journal of Near Eastern Studies*, 74, 189–96.

Haring, B. (2018). *From Single Sign to Pseudo-Script: An Ancient Egyptian System of Workmen's Identity Marks*. Leiden: Brill.

Haring, B. (2020). Ancient Egypt and the earliest known stages of alphabetic writing. In Ph. Boyes & Ph. Steele, eds., *Understanding Relations between Scripts II. Early Alphabets*. Oxford: Oxbow Books, pp. 53–67.

Haring, B. & Kaper, O. E., eds. (2009). *Pictograms or Pseudo Script? Non-textual Identity Marks in Practical Use in Ancient Egypt and Elsewhere: Proceedings of a Conference in Leiden, 19–20 December 2006*. Leiden: Nederlands Instituut voor het Nabije Oosten and Peeters.

Harris, R. (1986). *The Origin of Writing*. London: Duckworth.

Harris, R. (1995). *Signs of Writing*. London: Routledge.

Hendrickx, S. (2008). Rough ware as an element of symbolism and craft specialisation at Hierakonpolis' elite cemetery HK6. In B. Midant-Reynes & Y. Tristant, eds., *Egypt at Its Origins 2. Proceedings of the International Conference 'Origin of the State: Predynastic and Early Dynastic Egypt', Toulouse (France), 5th–8th September 2005*. Leuven: Uitgeverij Peeters & Departement Oosterse Studies, pp. 61–85.

Hoch, J. E. (1994). *Semitic Words in Egyptian Texts of the New Kingdom and Third Intermediate Period*. Princeton, NJ: Princeton University Press.

Hornung, E., Krauss R. & Warburton, D. A., eds., *Ancient Egyptian Chronology*. Leiden: Brill.

Houston, S. & Stauder, A. (2020). What is a hieroglyph? *L'homme: Revue française d'anthropologie*, 233, 9–44.

Iversen, E. (1993). *The Myth of Egypt and Its Hieroglyphs in European Tradition*. 2nd ed. Princeton, NJ: Princeton University Press.

Johnson, J. (1991). *Thus Wrote 'Onchsheshonqy: An Introductory Grammar of Demotic.* 2nd ed. Chicago, IL: Oriental Institute of the University of Chicago.

Junge, F. (2008). *Neuägyptisch. Einführung in die Grammatik.* 3rd ed. Wiesbaden: Harrassowitz.

Kahl, J. (1992). Die Defektivschreibungen in den Pyramidentexten. *Lingua Aegyptia*, 2, 99–116.

Kahl, J. & Shafik, S. (2021). *Gottesworte in Assiut: Eine Paläographie der relifierten Monumentalhieroglyphen der Ersten Zwischenzeit und der 12. Dynastie.* Wiesbaden: Harrassowitz.

Kammerzell, F. (2001). Die Entstehung der Alphabetreihe: Zum ägyptischen Ursprung der semitischen und westlichen Schriften. In D. Borchers, F. Kammerzell & S. Weninger, eds., *Hieroglyphen, Alphabete, Schriftreformen: Studien zu Multiliteralismus, Schriftwechsel und Orthographieneuregelungen.* Gottingen: Seminar für Ägyptologie und Koptologie, pp. 117–58.

Kammerzell, F. (2009). Defining non-textual marking systems, writing, and other systems of graphic information processing. In P. Andrássy, J. Budka & F. Kammerzell, eds., *Non-textual Marking Systems, Writing and Pseudo Script from Prehistory to Modern Times.* Gottingen: Seminar für Ägyptologie und Koptologie, pp. 277–308.

Kaplony, P. (1963). *Die Inschriften der ägyptischen Frühzeit III.* Wiesbaden: Harrassowitz.

Keel, O. (2004). Some of the earliest groups of locally produced scarabs from Palestine. In M. Bietak & E. Czerny, eds., *Scarabs of the Second Millennium BC from Egypt, Nubia, Crete and the Levant: Chronological and Historical Implications.* Vienna: Verlag der Österreichischen Akademie der Wissenschaften, pp. 73–101.

Keller, C. A. (2001). A family affair: the decoration of Theban Tomb 359. In W. V. Davies ed., *Colour and Painting in Ancient Egypt.* London: British Museum Press, pp. 73–93.

Kilani, M. (2019). *Vocalisation in Group Writing: A New Proposal.* Hamburg: Widmaier.

Kitchen, K. A. (1979). *Ramesside Inscriptions: Historical and Biographical.* Vol. II. Oxford: B. H. Blackwell.

Klotz, D. (2020). The enigmatic frieze of Ramesses II at Luxor temple. In D. Klotz & A. Stauder, eds., *Enigmatic Writing in the New Kingdom I: Revealing, Transforming, and Display in Egyptian Hieroglyphs.* Berlin: De Gruyter, pp. 49–99.

Klotz, D. & Brown, M. W. (2016). The enigmatic statuette of Djehutymose (MFA 24.743): deputy of Wawat and viceroy of Kush. *Journal of the American Research Center in Egypt* 52, 269–302.

Kopetzky, K. (2018). Tell el-Dab'a and Byblos: new chronological evidence. *Ägypten und Levante* 28, 309–58.

Kruchten, J.-M. (1999). Traduction et commentaire des inscriptions. In N. Cherpion, *Deux tombes de la XVIIIe dynastie à Deir el-Medina: Nos 340 (Amenemhat) et 354 (anonyme)*. Cairo: Institut Français d'Archéologie Orientale, pp. 41–55.

Laboury, D. (2013). L'artiste égyptien, ce grand méconnu de l'égyptologie. In G. Andreu-Lanoë, ed., *L'art du contour: Le dessin dans l'Égypte ancienne*. Paris: Musée du Louvre and Somogy éditions d'art, pp. 28–35.

Laboury, D. (2020). Designers and makers of Ancient Egyptian monumental epigraphy. In V. Davies & D. Laboury, eds., *The Oxford Handbook of Egyptian Epigraphy and Palaeography*. New York: Oxford University Press, pp. 84–101.

Laboury, D. (2022a). Le signe comme image … ou l'image comme signe. In S. Polis, ed., *Guide des écritures de l'Égypte ancienne*. Cairo: Institut Français d'Archéologie Orientale, pp. 144–53.

Laboury, D. (2022b). Artistes et écriture hiéroglyphique dans l'Égypte des pharaons. *Bulletin de la Société française d'égyptologie*, 207, 37–67.

Leal, P. G. (2014). Reassessing Horapollo: a contemporary view on *Hieroglyphika*. *Emblematica*, 21, 37–75.

Leitz, C. (2001). Die beiden kryptographischen Inschriften aus Esna mit den Widdern und Krokodillen. *Studien zur Altägyptischen Kultur*, 29, 251–76.

Leitz, C. (2003). Der ägyptische Tempel und die ptolemäische Hieroglyphenschrift: ein Medium ganz besonderer Art. In H. von Hesber & W. Thiel, eds., *Medien in der Antike: Kommunikative Qualität und normative Wirkung*. Cologne: Lehr- und Forschungszentrum für die antiken Kulturen des Mittelmeerraumes der Universität zu Köln, pp. 69–92.

Leitz, C. (2009). *Quellentexte zur ägyptischen Religion I: Die Tempelinschriften der griechisch-römischen Zeit*. 3rd ed. Berlin: Lit Verlag Dr. W. Hopf.

Lincke, E.-S. & Kammerzell, F. (2012). Egyptian classifiers at the interface of lexical semantics and pragmatics. In E. Grossman, S. Polis & J. Winand, eds., *Lexical Semantics in Egyptian*. Hamburg: Widmaier, pp. 55–112.

Loprieno, A. (1995). *Ancient Egyptian: A Linguistic Introduction*. Cambridge: Cambridge University Press.

McDowell, A. (1993). *Hieratic Ostraca in the Hunterian Museum Glasgow (The Colin Campbell Ostraca)*. Oxford: Griffith Institute.

Meeks, D. (2015). Linguistique et égyptologie: Entre théorisation à priori et contribution à l'étude de la culture égyptienne. *Chronique d'Égypte* 179, 40–67.

Meeks, D. (2021). L'écriture énigmatique égyptienne est-elle énigmatique? *Bibliotheca Orientalis* 78, 552–68.

Montet, P. (1928). Notes et documents pour servir à l'histoire des relations entre l'ancienne Égypte et la Syrie. *Kêmi* 1, 83–93.

Morenz, L. (2004). *Bild-Buchstaben und symbolische Zeichen: Die Heraus*bildung *der Schrift in der hohen Kultur Altägyptens*. Fribourg: Academic Press and Vandenhoeck & Ruprecht.

Morenz, L. (2009). Sakrale Motiviertheit alphabetischer Zeichenwelten: Bildhaft-Kanaanäisch, Meroitisch-Hieroglypisch und eine gräko-ägyptische, hieroglyphische Alphabetschrift. In B. Haring & O. Kaper, eds., *Pictograms or Pseudo Script? Non-textual Identity Marks in Practical Use in Ancient Egypt and Elsewhere. Proceedings of a Conference in Leiden, 19–20 December 2006*. Leiden: Nederlands Instituut voor het Nabije Oosten and Peeters, pp. 199–210.

Morenz, L. (2011). *Die Genese der Alphabetschrift: Ein Markstein ägyptisch-kanaanäischer Kulturkontakte*. Wurzburg: Ergon.

Morenz, L. (2019). *Sinai und Alphabetschrift: Die frühesten alphabetischen Inschriften und ihr kanaanäisch-ägyptischer Entstehungshorizont im Zweiten Jahrtausend v. Chr.* Berlin: EB-Verlag Dr. Brandt.

Näser, C. (2001). Zur Interpretation funerärer Praktiken im Neuen Reich: Der Ostfriedhof von Deir el-Medine. In C. Arnst, I. Hafemann & A. Lohwasser, eds., *Begegnungen. Antike Kulturen im Niltal: Festgabe für Erika Endesfelder, Karl-Heinz Priese, Walter Friedrich Reineke, Steffen Wenig, von Schülern und Mitarbeitern*. Leipzig: Verlag Helmar Wodtke und Katharina Stegbauer, pp. 373–98.

Nöth, W. (1990). *Handbook of Semiotics*. Bloomington: Indiana University Press.

Parker, H. (2022). The proto-Sinaitic inscriptions at Serabit el-Khadim in their archaeological context: date and function. *Ägypten und Levante* 32, 269–311.

Parkinson, R. (1999). *Cracking Codes: The Rosetta Stone and Decipherment*. London: British Museum Press.

Perego, E. (2013). The other writing: iconic literacy and situla art in pre-Roman Veneto (Italy). In K. E. Piquette & R. D. Whitehouse, eds., *Writing As Material Practice: Substance, Surface and Medium*. London: Ubiquity Press, pp. 253–70.

Petrie, W. (1909). *Qurneh*. London: School of Archaeology in Egypt and Bernard Quaritch.

Peust, C. (1999). *Egyptian Phonology: An Introduction to the Phonology of a Dead Language*. Gottingen: Peust & Gutschmidt.

Peust, C. (2016). Der Lautwert der Schilfblatt-Hieroglyphe (M 17). *Lingua Aegyptia*, 24, 89–100.

Pietri, R. (2022). Écrire et lire des statues. In S. Polis, ed., *Guide des écritures de l'Égypte ancienne*. Cairo: Institut Français d'Archéologie Orientale, pp. 154–7.

Polis, S. & Rosmorduc, S. (2015). The hieroglyphic sign functions: suggestions for a revised taxonomy. In H. Amstutz, A. Dorn, M. Müller, M. Ronsdorf & S. Uljas, eds., *Fuzzy Boundaries: Festschrift für Antonio Loprieno*. Hamburg: Widmaier, pp. 149–74.

Posener, G. (1969). Sur les inscriptions pseudo-hiéroglyphiques de Byblos. *Mélanges de l'Université Saint-Joseph*, 45, 223–39.

Quack, J. F. (2010). Difficult hieroglyphs and unreadable Demotic? How the Ancient Egyptians dealt with the complexities of their script. In A. de Voogt & I. Finkel, eds., *The Idea of Writing: Play and Complexity*. Leiden: Brill, pp. 235–51.

Quack, J. F. (2017). How the Coptic script came about. In E. Grossmann, P. Dils, T. Richter & W. Schenkel, eds., *Greek Influence on Egyptian-Coptic*. Hamburg: Widmaier, pp. 27–96.

Rampersad, S. (2020). Commodity branding and textual potmarks: Three bread mould intaglios from Tell Gabbara. *Journal of Egyptian Archaeology*, 106, 187–98.

Raven, M. J. (1991). *The Tomb of Iurudef: A Memphite Official in the Reign of Ramesses II*. Leiden: National Museum of Antiquities Leiden and Egypt Exploration Society.

Ray, J. (1994). Literacy and language in Egypt in the Late and Persian Periods. In A. K. Bowman & G. Woolf, eds., *Literacy and Power in the Ancient World*. Cambridge: Cambridge University Press, pp. 51–66.

Regulski, I. (2010). A palaeographic study of early writing in Egypt. Leuven: Uitgeverij Peeters & Departement Oosterse Studies.

Richards, F. (2001). *The Anra Scarab: An Archaeological and Historical Approach*. Oxford: Archaeopress.

Rilly, C. (2022). Meroitic writing. In W. Wendrich, A. Stauder, D. Agut-Labordère et al., eds., *UCLA Encyclopedia of Egyptology*. https://escholarship.org/uc/item/2ts0n9p0.

Rilly, C. & De Voogt, A. (2012). *The Meroitic Language and Writing System*. Cambridge: Cambridge University Press.

Roberson, J. A. (2020). *Enigmatic Writing in the New Kingdom II: A Lexikon of Ancient Egyptian Cryptography of the New Kingdom*. Berlin: De Gruyter.

Robertson, J. S. (2004). The possibility and actuality of writing. In S. Houston, ed., *The First Writing: Script Invention As History and Process.* Cambridge: Cambridge University Press, pp. 16–38.

Roth, A. M. (1991). *Egyptian Phyles in the Old Kingdom: The Evolution of a System of Social Organization.* Chicago, IL: Oriental Institute of the University of Chicago.

Rzepka, S. (2015). 'Funny signs' graffiti vs. textual graffiti: contemporary or not? In J. Budka, F. Kammerzell & S. Rzepka, eds., *Non-textual Marking Systems in Ancient Egypt (and Elsewhere).* Hamburg: Widmaier, pp. 159–83.

Sartori, M. (2022). Talking images: a semiotic and visual analysis of three Eighteenth-Dynasty chapels at Deir el-Medina (TT8, TT340, TT354). In S. Töpfer, P. del Vesco & F. Poole, eds., *Deir el-Medina through the Kaleidoscope: Proceedings of the International Workshop Turin 8th–10th October 2018.* Medina: Franco Cosimo Panini Editore S.p.A. https://formazio neericerca.museoegizio.it/en/pubblicazioni/deir-el-medina-en, pp. 651–76.

Sass, B. (1988). *The Genesis of the Alphabet and Its Development in the Second Millennium B.C.* Wiesbaden: Harrassowitz.

Sass, B. (2005). *The Genesis of the Alphabet and Its Development in the Second Millennium B.C.* twenty years later. *De Kêmi à Birît Nâri,* 2, 147–66.

Sass, B. (2019). The pseudo-hieroglyphic inscriptions from Byblos, their elusive dating, and their affinities with the early Phoenician inscriptions. In P. Abrahami & L. Battini, eds., *Ina ᵈmarri u qan ṭuppi. Par la bêche et le stylet! Cultures et sociétés syro-mésopotamiennes. Mélanges offerts à Olivier Rouault.* Oxford: Archaeopress, pp. 157–80.

Schenkel, W. (1994). Zur Formenbildung des Verbs im Neuägyptischen. *Orientalia,* 63, 10–15.

Schweitzer, S. D. (2003). Zur Herkunft der spätzeitlichen alphabetischen Schreibungen. In S. Bickel & A. Loprieno, eds., *Basel Egyptology Prize 1: Junior Research in Egyptian History, Archaeology, and Philology.* Basel: Schwabe & Company, pp. 371–86.

Soliman, D. (2015). Workmen's marks in pre-Amarna tombs at Deir el-Medina. In J. Budka, F. Kammerzell & S. Rzepka, eds., *Non-textual Marking Systems in Ancient Egypt (and Elsewhere).* Hamburg: Widmaier, pp. 109–32.

Soliman, D. (2018a). Ostraca with identity marks and the organisation of the royal necropolis workmen of the 18th Dynasty. *Bulletin de l'Institut français d'archéologie orientale* 118, 465–534.

Soliman, D. (2018b). Two groups of Deir el-Medina ostraca recording duty rosters and daily deliveries composed with identity marks. In R. Ast, M. Choat, J. Cromwell, J. Lougovaya & R. Yuen-Collingridge, eds,

*Observing the Scribe at Work: Scribal Practice in the Ancient World*. Leuven: Peeters, pp. 45–61.

Stauder, A. (2020). The visual otherness of the enigmatic text in some netherworld books of the New Kingdom. In D. Klotz & A. Stauder, eds., *Enigmatic Writing in the New Kingdom I: Revealing, Transforming, and Display in Egyptian Hieroglyphs*. Berlin: De Gruyter, pp. 249–65.

Stauder, A. (2022). Paths to early phoneticism: Egyptian writing in the late fourth millennium BCE. In L. Morenz, A. Stauder & B. Büma, eds., *Wege zur frühen Schrift: Niltal und Zweistromenland*. Berlin: EB-Verlag Dr. Brandt.

Tallet, P. (2012). *La zone minière du Sud-Sinaï I: Catalogue complémentaire des inscriptions du Sinaï*. 2 vols. Cairo: Institut Français d'Archéologie Orientale.

Teissier, B. (1996). *Egyptian Iconography on Syro-Palestinian Cylinder Seals of the Middle Bronze Age*. Fribourg: University Press and Vandenhoeck & Ruprecht.

Thiers, C. (2022). L'écriture ptolemaïque. In S. Polis, ed., *Guide des écritures de l'Égypte ancienne*, Cairo: Institut Français d'Archéologie Orientale, pp. 52–7.

Töpfer, S., del Vesco, P. & Poole, F., eds. (2022). *Deir el-Medina through the Kaleidoscope: Proceedings of the International Workshop Turin 8th–10th October 2018*. Medina: Franco Cosimo Panini Editore S.p.A. https://forma zioneericerca.museoegizio.it/en/pubblicazioni/deir-el-medina-en.

Valbelle, D., (1985). *'Les ouvriers de la Tombe': Deir el-Médineh à l'époque ramesside*. Cairo: Institut Français d'Archéologie Orientale.

Van Soldt, W. (2013). The extent of literacy in Syria and Palestine during the second millennium B.C.E. In L. Feliu, A. M. Albà & J. Llop & J. San Martín, eds., *Time and History in the Ancient Near East*. Winona Lake, IN: Eisenbrauns, pp. 19–31.

Vandier d'Abbadie, J. & Jourdain, G. (1939). *Deux tombes de Deir el-Médineh. I. La chapelle de Khâ. II La tombe du scribe royal Amenemopet*. Cairo: Institut Français d'Archéologie Orientale.

Verner, M. (1982). *Altägyptische Särge in den Museen und Sammlungen der Tschechoslowakei, Lieferung 1*. Prague: Univerzita Karlova.

Vernus, P. (1991). Sur les graphies de la formule 'l'offrande que donne le roi' au Moyen Empire et à la Deuxième Période Intermediaire. In S. Quirke, ed., *Middle Kingdom Studies*. New Malden: SIA Publishing, pp. 141–52.

Vernus, P. (2015). Écriture hiéroglyphique égyptienne et écriture proto-sinaïtique: une typologie comparée. Acrophonie 'forte' et acrophonie 'faible'. In C. Rico & C. Attucci, eds., *Origins of the Alphabet: Proceedings of the First Polis Institute Interdisciplinary Conference*. Newcastle upon Tyne: Cambridge Scholars, pp. 142–75.

Vernus, P. (2016). La naissance de l'écriture dans l'Égypte pharaonique: une problématique revisitée. *Archéo-Nil*, 26, 105–34.

Vita, J.-P. & Zamora, J.-A. (2018). The Byblos script. In S. Ferrara and M. Valério, eds., *Paths into Script Formation in the Ancient Mediterranean*. Rome: Edizioni Qasar, pp. 75–102.

Vittmann, G. (2022). Eine pseudohieratische Gefäßinschrift der Spätzeit aus Deir el-Bahari (Kairo JE 56283). In B. Bryan, M. Smith & C. Di Cerbo et al., eds., *One Who Loves Knowledge: Studies in Honor of Richard Jasnow*. Columbus, GA: Lockwood Press, pp. 467–92.

Von Lieven, A. (2009). Script and pseudo scripts in Graeco-Roman Egypt. In P. Andrássy, J. Budka & F. Kammerzell, eds., *Non-textual Marking Systems, Writing and Pseudo Script from Prehistory to Modern Times*. Gottingen: Seminar für Ägyptologie und Koptologie, pp. 101–11.

Wente, E. F. (2001). Hieratic. In D. B. Redford, ed., *The Oxford Encyclopedia of Ancient Egypt*. Vol. 3. Oxford: Oxford University Press, pp. 206–10.

Werning, D. A. (2022). L'écriture énigmatique: distanciée, cryptique, sportive. In S. Polis, ed., *Guide des écritures de l'Égypte ancienne*. Cairo: Institut Français d'Archéologie Orientale, pp. 200–7.

Willems, H. (2018). Cylinder seals for the lower classes. *Zeitschrift für ägyptische Sprache und Altertumskunde*, 145, 187–204.

Wilson-Wright, A. (2013). Interpreting the Sinaitic inscriptions in context: a new reading of Sinai 345. *Hebrew Bible and Ancient Israel*, 2, 136–48.

Wilson-Wright, A. (2020). 'Beloved of the lady are those who . . . ': a recurring memorial formula in the Sinaitic inscriptions. *Bulletin of the American Schools of Oriental Research*, 384, 133–58.

Wimmer, S. (2008a). A new hieratic ostracon from Ashkelon. *Tel Aviv*, 35, 65–72.

Wimmer, S. (2008b). *Palästinisches Hieratisch: Die Zahl- und Sonderzeichen in der althebräischen Schrift*. Wiesbaden: Harrassowitz.

Winand, J. (1992). *Études de néo-égyptien, 1. La morphologie verbale*. Liège: Centre Informatique de Philosophie et Lettres.

Yamada, A. (2017). Some remarks on the evolution of the workers organization of the pyramid construction in the Old Kingdom: through the examination of the so-called mason's mark. In M. Bárta, F. Coppens & J. Krejčí, eds., *Abusir and Saqqara in the Year 2015*. Prague: Faculty of Arts, Charles University, pp. 489–501.

# Acknowledgements

I wish to thank the editors of the Elements series 'Ancient Egypt in Context' for inviting me to contribute this volume, and Cambridge University Press for including it in the series. Andréas Stauder has kindly read the manuscript before submission; Olaf Kaper has read a draft of Section 3.2. I wish to thank both of them, as well as the anonymous peer reviewers, for their comments, suggestions and additional references. My English has been polished by Elizabeth Bettles. Any remaining flaws are entirely my own. The hieroglyphic type used is JSesh (https://jsesh.qenherkhopeshef.org/).

Cambridge Elements

# Ancient Egypt in Context

## Gianluca Miniaci
*University of Pisa*
Gianluca Miniaci is Associate Professor in Egyptology at the University of Pisa, Honorary Researcher at the Institute of Archaeology, UCL–London, and Chercheur associé at the École Pratique des Hautes Études, Paris. He is currently co-director of the archaeological mission at Zawyet Sultan (Menya, Egypt). His main research interest focuses on the social history and the dynamics of material culture in the Middle Bronze Age Egypt and its interconnections between the Levant, Aegean, and Nubia.

## Juan Carlos Moreno García
*CNRS, Paris*
Juan Carlos Moreno García (PhD in Egyptology, 1995) is a CNRS senior researcher at the University of Paris IV–Sorbonne, as well as lecturer on social and economic history of ancient Egypt at the École des Hautes Études en Sciences Sociales (EHESS) in Paris. He has published extensively on the administration, socio-economic history, and landscape organization of ancient Egypt, usually in a comparative perspective with other civilizations of the ancient world, and has organized several conferences on these topics.

## Anna Stevens
*University of Cambridge and Monash University*
Anna Stevens is a research archaeologist with a particular interest in how material culture and urban space can shed light on the lives of the non-elite in ancient Egypt. She is Senior Research Associate at the McDonald Institute for Archaeological Research and Assistant Director of the Amarna Project (both University of Cambridge).

## About the Series

The aim of this Elements series is to offer authoritative but accessible overviews of foundational and emerging topics in the study of ancient Egypt, along with comparative analyses, translated into a language comprehensible to non-specialists. Its authors will take a step back and connect ancient Egypt to the world around, bringing ancient Egypt to the attention of the broader humanities community and leading Egyptology in new directions.

Cambridge Elements ⹀

# Ancient Egypt in Context

Printed in the United States
by Baker & Taylor Publisher Services